Ordinary Freedom

About the Author

Jon Bernie is a contemporary spiritual teacher in the lineage of Adyashanti, leading regular classes, retreats and intensives in the San Francisco Bay Area and beyond. As a counselor in private practice, Jon also works with individuals directly to facilitate consciousness development and deep emotional healing. A lifelong resident of the Bay Area, Jon has been at various times a Zero Balancing practitioner, a teacher of the Alexander Technique, a concert violinist and an ordained Zen Buddhist monk.

Jon's spiritual journey began with a spontaneous awakening experience at age sixteen, which led him to spend many years practicing in the Zen and Theravada Buddhist traditions, first as a monk in the lineage of Shunryu Suzuki-roshi, and later as an early student of Jack Kornfield. In the late 1980s, Jon's spiritual trajectory was profoundly altered when he met Advaita master Jean Klein, with whom he studied intensively for an extended period. Jon subsequently spent time with H.W.L. Poonja and Robert Adams, both direct disciples of Ramana Maharshi. Jon's spiritual development was also greatly aided by Brother David Steindl-Rast, a Benedictine monk who studied with several well-known Zen masters and has since been instrumental in building interfaith networks worldwide. After Jon met Adyashanti in 2002, his journey came to fruition, and subsequently Adya asked Jon to teach.

Clear Water Sangha

Clear Water Sangha, a non-profit organization, was established to support the teachings of Jon Bernie. The board of directors and dedicated volunteers help coordinate a variety of activities including the production of written publications, management of satsangs, retreats and other events, and ongoing maintenance of Jon's website.

For further information, please visit:
www.sf-satsang.org

Praise for Ordinary Freedom

To find an accomplished spiritual teacher is a rare gift. To find a book that puts you in a most lively way in the presence of such a teacher is even more rare. But here it is! Jon Bernie's Ordinary Freedom *has all the power of the spoken word and vibrates with the overtones of that teacher's caring, compassionate nearness. Deep, yet always simple; simple, yet never simplistic; clear, eloquent, and always to the point,* Ordinary Freedom *is not an ordinary book. It springs from freedom and breathes freedom.* ***Caution:*** *This book may be hazardous to your current level of consciousness!*

Brother David Steindl-Rast, OSB, author, lecturer, co-founder of www.gratefulness.org

What a beautiful, simple, heartfelt message! The end of seeking is not something to be found in the future—it is right here, present at the very heart of experience, just waiting to be discovered by those who are ready and willing to come face-to-face with life.

Jon Bernie expresses the timeless truth of non-duality (non-separation) in such a warm, authentically human voice. He meets you as a wise, loving friend—rather than as spiritual master or guru—and gently points out the various ways in which you are currently at war with your own experience. His message is rare and precious in that it does not attempt to deny or transcend our humanity, or dismiss it as an aberration, but rather embraces it fully as part of an infinitely bigger picture. Jon honours your embodied experience, whilst at the same time clearly and directly pointing you far beyond the personal, to a wordless freedom that belongs to no-one, and therefore is available to everyone.

Read Ordinary Freedom *and rediscover something that you have always known—that this seemingly ordinary life is already the miracle you've been seeking, and that here and now is forever saturated with wonder. This is mature, grounded spirituality for grown-ups, and I thoroughly recommend it.*

Jeff Foster, author of *The Wonder of Being* and *An Extraordinary Absence.*

Ordinary Freedom

Jon Bernie

NON-DUALITY PRESS

UNITED KINGDOM

Ordinary Freedom

First edition published July 2010 by Non-Duality Press

Cover photo taken by Jon Bernie at his former retreat in Bolinas.

Non-Duality Press is an Imprint of

newharbingerpublications, inc.

5674 Shattuck Avenue • Oakland CA 94609 • USA

800-748-6273 • fax 510-652-5472

www.newharbinger.com

Softcover edition

ISBN: 978-0-9563091-9-8

www.newharbinger.com

Dedication

I want to dedicate this book to my Mom, who taught me to trust my feelings and question everything; and to my Dad, who was my first Zen Master.

Contents

Foreword

We do not usually think of ordinariness and spirituality as existing together, and in one sense they do not belong together. If we think that spiritual freedom is something that can fit nicely into our ordinary way of viewing life, with all its division and conflict, we are sorely mistaken. Spiritual freedom comes about through a deep reorientation of the way we perceive, not only ourselves, but all of life. However, if we view ordinary as referring to a change of perception available to anyone, right here and now, then spiritual freedom is indeed ordinary. Freedom is also ordinary in the sense of being permeated by a state of openness, naturalness and ease; and it is these qualities that characterize Jon Bernie's teachings.

This wonderful collection of Jon's teachings really captures his ability to point us back to our own innate freedom. What makes Jon's teachings so powerful and relevant, though, is that no part of the human experience is denied. Indeed, there is an open encouragement for all of our human experience to be included and embraced as a means of discovering the infinite ground of being within which all of our experience unfolds. This in itself is a great gift to any spiritual seeker looking to find out what freedom is really all about. But if you read through these teachings with all of your senses open and alert you will begin to intuit something more.

You will begin to notice a deep silence taking form within you. Not a relative silence that is simply the absence of sound, but a silence that is a deep and welcoming presence. This silent presence is like discovering a radiant thread of truth running inside of you. It has always been there of course, but you may not have noticed it or given it your full attention. Because giving our full attention to something other than our wandering minds is not something we are encouraged to do very often. But if you are alert with every part of your being not only may you be given the gift of a truly wise and compassionate spiritual teaching but you may be drawn into the heart of a perfect stillness where Jon's words will pierce you, and like two arrows meeting in mid-air, your world will stop. And in a single breathless instant radiance may find you and eternity will be yours.

Adyashanti
San Francisco, May 2010

Introduction

I remember being four years old, looking up at the stars, and wondering, "What's going on here?" At the age of eleven, I found myself arguing with my Sunday school teacher about the existence of God. I wasn't buying it. I came home and declared to my mother, "I'm not going to Sunday school anymore, I'm too busy practicing the violin!" "Okay, honey", she replied. I became an agnostic, saying at the time, "When I see God, I'll believe it." I assumed then that most of my friends, in their various religions, were being brainwashed.

During my teenage years, struggling with the meaning of existence, I began an inner search that led to a spiritual awakening around the age of sixteen. At the time, I did not know what had happened to me, and it would be quite a while before I found out. I had unknowingly tapped into the mystery of existence, and that encounter not only changed the course of my life, but ultimately led to the end of my struggle with "what is." It led to the end of seeking, the end of fear, and the end of self-identification, all of which are ways of saying that it led to the discovery and realization that what we fundamentally are is conscious energy and space, or awareness itself. This realization is called Freedom.

This book is about Freedom. It's not about a special state or condition called "Freedom," some idea or concept to be believed in; rather, it is about the recognition and realization of our essential nature. When we arrive in this moment and awaken to the truth of our existence, we discover that Freedom is completely ordinary. Ordinary, yet awesome.

The recognition and realization of our essential nature is for many a gradual transition. The challenge of our generation is to find out how to support this transformation in the midst of our ordinary lives.

Jon Bernie

Your every step
leads not away from it.

Dōgen

Being Here

Awakening in its essence is simply *being here*. It's not the thought, "being here," or a story you tell yourself internally: "*I'm* being here." There is no thinker or storyteller. There is no *one* who is being here.

Awakening is not about belief, or even about understanding, at least not in the way we usually think of understanding. It's tricky to talk about. It's easy to understand why practitioners in many monastic traditions remain in silence most of the time. With talking removed from the equation, you can just do what you have to do—chop wood, carry water, plant seeds, pick vegetables—in that kind of environment, things can become very, very simple.

But even out here in the world, in the midst of our busy lives, that simplicity is still available. You can simply attend to your immediate experience in this moment. You don't need to understand it, or believe anything about it. Just be here with what is, as it is. And as your experience becomes increasingly simple, you drop even that story, the story of it being simple. You freefall into openness, into emptiness.

~

Awakening is about letting go of all control. That's why meditation practice can be useful for our physical bodies, which are conditioned to control, and defend, and hold on. Meditation can help you notice where the *holding on* is. You just sit, and stop, and notice what's going on physically, emotionally, energetically. The physical body is a wonderful mirror.

Editor's Note: *These talks and dialogs were adapted from transcripts of Jon's public meetings (usually referred to as satsang — literally, "meeting in truth") and retreats from 2006 to 2009.*

So just be here. Notice what's going on. You don't need to analyze it, fix it, figure it out or explain it. Awakening is what's left when all that falls away. It is literally dropping everything, and just being here. Conceptually, it's tremendously simple. It is simplicity itself: just being. Now you're no longer trying to get anywhere; you no longer experience that compulsion. You're like the sun—grounded in radiant presence, connected to everything.

As you drop further into the awakening process, you begin to realize that everything—everything!—is simultaneously transmitting and receiving awakening. And as you give your attention to *that,* to that amazing process, there's a sense of deepening, and an awareness of a kind of power or energy that's present everywhere; and gradually you become that energy.

~

It's not necessary, however, to believe any of this. All that's required is attention, and the willingness to let go of control. Whatever your experience is, that's what's happening—*let it.* Whatever you're facing right now—whether you're feeling open or shut down, whether you're at peace or struggling—*that* is the doorway. You have the opportunity to open to what is being given *right now,* what is arising *right now* in the mirror of your attention. The experience of life is always a reflection, and that itself is the ultimate teaching, if you're ready to receive it.

Walking the Path

When we gather together in satsang, the true teaching is really the silence. It's not about the teacher's personality, or the student's. As Jean Klein used to say, it's when there's no one taking themselves to be a teacher and no one taking themselves to be a student that true teaching takes place.

The truth is, we're not separate at all. We're the same. When we're caught in our personal struggles, it does feel like we're separate, it does feel like we're different; and of course in the human, physical sense, we are. But in our essence, in the fundamental reality of that which we are, we are not separate. The silence is an opportunity to open to that.

It's not about belief, thank goodness. We'd be in real trouble if it were. Our beliefs are the cause of all the grief! The more tightly we hold on to our beliefs, the more we hurt. That's what suffering is, that holding on. That's all the illusion of separateness is, too. But that holding on is really just self-protection—it's the human organism trying to survive and be comfortable. As you know if you're familiar with psychology, humans develop a variety of strategies for surviving. We call those strategies ego, or personality, and it's easy to be fooled into thinking that our personality is who we are. But who we *truly* are is no one. We're just openness; just freedom.

There's nothing I need to teach you, actually. Just pay attention to what's present. If you simply allow what's coming up to come up, and you don't resist it, then it's not a problem—it can move through the organism and be fully experienced. And if you do experience it as a problem, then open to *that* experience: the tension, the struggle, the resistance. Allow yourself to feel that discomfort. Allow it to be fully encountered so it can move through you without sticking.

Amazingly, all you need to learn is simply to be available to what is. That's all that's required. But instead we often tend to go, "I want this, but not that. I want the bliss, the oneness, the joy; but I don't want the pain, the fear, the grief, the anger." Ironically, a lot of so-called teaching is just pointing out that *not wanting*.

It's not the experience itself—pain, fear, whatever—that's the problem. It's the resistance to that experience: the trying to get rid of it, the trying to fix it, the trying to understand it. I call that the *primary resistance*. That resistance is usually unconscious, but it can come to the surface if you're willing to really stay with your experience. That's actually all that's required, just hanging in there. Of course that can sometimes be more challenging than it sounds, because it can often be a very bumpy ride.

But as you gradually become more and more available to the truth of who you are, you'll find that "hanging in there" is just what naturally happens. At first, allowing what is may seem to require effort; but as you become established in awareness you'll find that what *really* takes effort is resisting, struggling with what is. When you can finally let go of *that* effort, then being with what is, whatever it is, becomes truly effortless.

I've often suggested that the most helpful attitudes to cultivate are those of the explorer and the scientist. The explorer wanders boldly in the unknown, always in new territory, never knowing what will be encountered next. The scientist observes what arises without any preconceived ideas about what's happening or what it means, and *questions everything*.

If you're identified with your beliefs, then questioning them is essential. Your beliefs are not true or false, or even good or bad; beliefs are just mental constructs. In the short run they're either useful or not useful, but ultimately they become irrelevant as you reach that stepping-off point when you're finally *just here*. Then belief is no longer what's going on. Your perspective has shifted. And gradually you learn to open to that shift and allow it to deepen, and eventually it's permanent. That's all. It happens by itself, really. No one does it for you. You don't even do it for yourself. If you could, you'd have done it already.

The path is really about honesty, too, about just telling it like it is, however it is. No shame, no blame. All that's required is that you honestly express the truth of where you're at in this moment. It doesn't matter whether it looks good or bad, or whether it feels good or bad. What's important is just putting it into the light, so to speak. The truth really will set you free — even the limited truth!

Often people are afraid of not being "spiritual" enough. You may, for instance, go through a period where a lot of difficult psychological material is emerging, where you're in what seems like a perpetually negative headspace, but find you're reluctant to acknowledge how you're feeling. Because it's not supposed to be like that, right? It's supposed to be like in the spiritual sales pitch, the shining oasis of light we're supposed to get to, et cetera. So you don't want to admit, maybe even to yourself, that what you're actually experiencing is enormous suffering.

But *who* is suffering? Who's angry? Who's afraid? Who's sad? Do you really have an answer for that? Ask yourself the question — and then stop, just sit there. Open to the question. Don't just ask the question; *be* the question.

Can you allow yourself to sit in the discomfort of your question, without having to have the answer? Can you *not know*? Can you open to *not knowing*? Of course! *Not knowing* is your nature. It's totally natural, like a flower emanating its fragrance. The flower doesn't try, that's just its nature. That's why nature is so beautiful; it's not trying to be beautiful, it just is. And that's really the beauty of that which we are, if we *just are*. It's enough.

Aliveness

Our true nature is to be fully alive. This aliveness is not something that one person has and another doesn't. It's not something one has to be worthy of. Aliveness is our essence, our true being. We may be oblivious to it; our aliveness may be obscured and heavily fortified over. We may be in the mode of just surviving and getting by, which is important for humans, obviously, and is often difficult.

But at some point we find we have the space to begin to let the unfolding and the transformation happen. And it does happen! Sometimes things shift suddenly and dramatically, but usually the change unfolds gradually, in stages, the way an acorn gradually becomes an oak tree.

There's really no end to this transformation. How could there be? The mystery keeps revealing itself. We never stop learning—if anything, we become more skilled at learning. We become better students, you might say. Ultimately there are no teachers, only students.

As we deepen in the mystery, our minds become open and available. We have fewer and fewer preconceived ideas about what's happening. We find the willingness in each moment to learn, to not be the knower. When we're truly open to this presence, we find we naturally open to it even more deeply. We enter into it and we receive it, profoundly. That's what transmission is. That's the mystery and magic and power of satsang.

Energy and Spirit

If you take some time to sit silently, in stillness, you'll perceive a range of different things. You may feel tired, sleepy; you may experience some physical discomfort; or you may find yourself restless, distracted. Maybe you'll discover you're going through something emotionally, something you might not otherwise have noticed. You'd think that sitting quietly would be a fairly easy thing to do, but actually, to sit consciously can be difficult or even overwhelming. And yet there's a power in the stillness. There's the possibility of opening to our fundamentally energetic nature.

In these kinds of discussions, I often prefer to use the word "energetic" rather than "spiritual." It's less encumbered with beliefs and concepts. Energy is practical—you flip the switch and the light goes on. We don't necessarily understand every detail of how it works, but we don't need to. We live with it, we accept it. It's part of our reality.

So from the perspective of awareness, whatever's being perceived, whether it's thought or feeling, sensation or emotion, is fundamentally a movement of energy. When we really awaken, we realize we're not separate from that energy. We begin to live *as* that movement, as that energy, and then we've transitioned into the unknown, into the mystery—into true aliveness.

At a certain point we don't even think about it any more; thinking about it falls away, and we're simply this presence, this awakeness, this ease of being. Awakening then shows us how to take care of the next moment. In Zen they say it doesn't matter how big your garden is, as long as you can take care of it. So you find out how to take care of it. You just do the next thing.

The next thing is what's right in front of us, right now. So often our attention is elsewhere—on something we're worrying about, or some set of future plans. To be able continually to bring ourselves back—*that* is the opportunity our practice offers. So we simply feel, we simply open to this presence, this energy that we fundamentally are, right now. We give our attention to the unknown, the unspeakable.

There are so many names for this mystery that we are: presence, spaciousness, emptiness, God, love, the Tao—it goes on and on and on. But once you've opened to it, once you've realized that you *are* that, forget all the names; just *be* that.

That doesn't mean you become spaced out on the divine and nonfunctional—that you can't drive a car, hammer a nail, install software, or whatever. Rather, you're able to do those things, to function in reality, much more richly and completely than ever before. There's no longer any separation between "me" and "my experience." So-called "my experience" is a mirage, a projection. When you're fully alive there is no more projection; there's only aliveness.

Dissolving Into Light

To awaken is to dissolve in one place and simultaneously appear everywhere. Awakening can also be called *being presence,* being energy. Karmic arisings, whatever their nature, are fuel for dissolving. So rather than resisting, or fighting, or arguing with what is—instead of all that, simply *accept* what is. Receive what is, allow what is. *Become* what is.

Now there's no separation between perceiver and perceived—there's just *being* perception. There's just listening, just observing, just feeling, just thinking. And you allow this gestation to happen, you allow this growth, as painful—or ecstatic!—as it might be.

Satsang can sometimes feel like being in a pressure cooker. It just gets hotter and hotter! So you let it get hotter, you let it get more amplified. That may be unsettling physically; you might even start shaking, or find you want to run out the door. As Robert Adams once said, if you've come here to hear a lecture you've come to the wrong place!

The good news is you don't have to understand how it works for it to work. Being here is enough. All you have to do is learn to allow yourself to cook. To be dissolved into light. To appear everywhere simultaneously. That is freedom.

~

Q. I'm feeling this intense heat lately. I'm very aware of this intense sense of trying, but I don't know what the trying is directed at.

How do you know you're trying? Is it a physical sensation, like a pressure or a pushing? Or is it a mental or emotional experience?

Q. It's more of an association I have. I don't even know what I'm trying to do anymore. I've been struggling to awaken for so long, and this tension is just cumulative. It doesn't even seem to have a direction anymore, it's just a buildup. And the more I look at it, the more the sensation seems to intensify.

That intensification may actually be the beginning of an expansion. See if you can just let it be for a while. Just sit with that pressure, but without expectation—that's the tricky part. Don't get in there with expectations or conclusions about how or why you're sitting with it. Put all that aside.

Like I said, it really is like cooking. And as with cooking, you also need to know when to take the lid off and let the pressure out. If you're steaming broccoli, you want to take it off the heat while it's still bright green, when it's softened, but before the heat has turned it completely limp. When I was a monk I used to sit these killer schedules—we never took the lid off!—and it was really too much. I found that out later when I left the monastery. Once I was living on my own, I could follow my own inner need to sit and be, and I found I'd go much deeper, and discover much more, when I wasn't pushing myself so hard.

Q. Just hearing you say that I get a little tense, because I've been wanting to know when to let the steam out, when to take the top off and when not to take the top off. What if I get it wrong? There's this uncomfortable sense that I don't know.

That's right, you don't know. So find out. Give yourself permission to experiment. Try more, try less. See what happens. Gradually you'll become sensitized to what best facilitates opening. Openness of the heart is our natural condition. It's love, and it's joy, and it's living life fully. It's what everyone wants, truly, and it's what we can have, each moment, once we allow ourselves to discover it. It just takes some time to find out how to let it blossom. So it's okay not to know. You're on the right track.

Being the Feeling

When you find yourself facing some difficult or unpleasant feeling, let yourself *be* that feeling. Don't be *with* the feeling, as a passive observer; rather, *be* the feeling itself. When you're being the feeling, there's no thinking. If you're being *with* the feeling there's still separation—there's "you," and there's "your feeling," which "you" are being with. There's still ego functioning, there's still someone having the feeling. But freedom is not for someone; freedom is for *no one.*

As long as there's someone having feelings, you're still identified. Identification is the source of suffering; it is the very definition of suffering. But when you're *being feeling,* there's no more identification. Once you drop the ego—that is, once you allow yourself to be fully present in this moment—there's no more somebody, no more identity, and no more suffering.

~

Q. I don't get this idea of being the feeling. I know how to receive feeling, and how to deny feeling, but I don't know what you mean by being it.

There's a merging that happens, if you will, of awareness with feeling, so that there's no longer "me" and "my feelings." The separation between them vanishes. That's also what I mean by being awareness. Same thing. Then emotion is no longer about the story we tell ourselves, it's just a movement, just this rush of energy moving through.

Q. The story fuels the emotion. And your advice is to let go of the story, or to somehow get underneath it?

The story is the surface; go to the source. The story may point to or help you access what's actually being felt, but it may have little to do with the true source of the feeling, except in some very limited sense. The movement of emotion can be all kinds of things, but it's very much a part of the human function. By itself it's not a problem. We make it into a problem when we block it, prevent it from fully moving. That causes all kinds of difficulties—mental, psychological, even physical.

Many people have to relearn how to feel, because during their lives they've learned to cope by separating from feeling, making it something "over there" that can be analyzed or dismissed. There's so much denial expertise out there. We're experts in maintaining unconsciousness! So how do we return to wholeness? Well, that's why people developed things like meditation, a way of getting into the body and really developing reflection; and conscious communication, sharing, expressing. There are so many methods to facilitate the healing.

But our focus here is awareness, so that's the perspective I want to speak from. People can develop a great deal of awareness and still maintain a certain degree of denial. This is a tricky area. The initial experience of awareness can be so pleasurable that it can itself become something you cling to as a defense against other, less pleasant kinds of experiences. I've sometimes called this "hiding in the light," and it can be one of the greatest detours on the spiritual journey.

People can also get very good at maintaining a certain high from being in spiritual environments where there's a lot of consciousness, or a lot of shakti. It can become a kind of habit—mainline a little shakti, right? Eventually, though, that no longer satisfies. You reach a certain spiritual maturity, where you're able to step up fully and take responsibility for following the truth itself, however it makes you feel.

As I've often said, the hardest part of getting to understanding is basically just hanging in there. But you learn to hang in there anyway, and at some point the question, "When am I going to get there?" isn't given much energy anymore. Instead of wondering when you'll arrive in some future moment, the question becomes, "How can I arrive fully in *this* moment?" That's all. In order to really transform, you have to enter the timeless, the now; the vastness of being; simple awareness itself.

Time is part of the illusion of separateness. When we're *being awareness*, our experience is timeless, seamless. And when separation dissolves—when *being awareness* is no longer something special, but just the way things are—then we're one with the truth, the divine, whatever you want to call it. That is the integration of the realization of who we truly are. When we're at peace, when we're in oneness, then nothing is lacking.

You begin to see how it *opens. How* it *does it.*
And then you find out how to let it.

Letting Go

Realizing our true self is *letting go.* That's really all it is—just letting go. And letting go happens in an infinite number of ways. You hear so many different stories of how the process unfolds, how it reveals itself for different people. But its essence is universal: simply letting go into this openness, this radiant vibrancy of pure consciousness.

We don't really know how letting go happens. We want to know so we can *make* it happen. We want to be able to facilitate it, and of course also avoid doing anything to hinder it. And that's completely reasonable! But gradually we find that letting go really isn't our job. Rather, our task is to learn how to let things be exactly as they are.

That's not to be confused with some kind of abdication of human responsibility. It doesn't mean letting your garbage pile up, or ignoring personal commitments. What it does mean is *simply being fully present,* right now, without pushing experience away, or pulling it toward you either. Pushing and pulling are manifestations of the ego function, ways of keeping the self defended. Letting go means relinquishing those defenses and allowing oneself to be open as consciousness, as presence, as vibrant aliveness.

So we find out how to let things be as they are, and gradually our limiting conditions fall away by themselves. As a famous Zen poem puts it,

Sitting quietly, doing nothing
Spring comes and the grass grows by itself

You just live your simple, ordinary life, and the falling away of identification happens by itself.

Finding the Balance

When the sense of "me" drops away, even for just a moment, that moment of awareness is a moment in which the ego's projections onto reality are ended. The filter between perception and reality is dropped. Reality is directly experienced. At the same time, there's no "knowing" of reality, no thinking about it. You're no longer "relating" to reality; you're *being* reality.

Being has a quality of openness, of ease—of balance. Lately I've found myself talking a lot about balance. So much of our search is really about finding that balance between pure awareness and our limited humanity. We often want to fix our humanity, or make it better. And of course there's nothing wrong with wanting to improve our humanity; that's just nature working on itself. But our essence, that which we truly are, is already perfect.

So how do we find that balance? When we experience those moments of non-projection, then we see—directly, clearly, honestly—things as they are. There may be unfinished business in one's heart, or pain in one's body that hasn't moved, and the quality of the attention we bring to those things is very important. That's why you often hear about the importance of compassion, of forgiveness. We may feel broken, as if we can't be fixed, and we need to have compassion for our own brokenness, or we can easily become lost in despair or hopelessness. But freedom is outside the realm of hope and hopelessness.

So we take responsibility for our humanness by really learning to take care of ourselves, and by really listening to what's present, even if we don't like it, even if it's painful. In that listening is amazing transformative power. When we give that kind of attention to our condition, it becomes saturated with energy and begins to move, begins to unravel. "Conditioned-ness," in its essence, is simply contraction, a kind of energetic held-ness.

But life in its essence is not held at all, and gradually we see that it's not even possible to hold onto life. Life is space, life is energy. And when we have those moments of connection, we're one with that space and energy. Maybe we call it bliss, or oneness, or unconditional love. I often call it *intimacy*. Because when we're open, there's no "you" and no "me." We literally feel each other as one. If you have tears, I have tears. There is no separation.

Transmission is happening in all directions, everywhere, all the time; it's infinitely multi-directional. So what we really realize is that as we're learning, we're also teaching. As we're being nourished, we're also nourishing. *That's* the flow of aliveness, the aliveness of the attention.

When we learn to really be with what is, then compassion is truly possible, and the movement of what has been held, or the healing of what has been wounded, can begin to happen. We can move into wakefulness, into happiness. Not some idea of happiness, but the real richness, the real joy of life, even with all its challenges and difficulties.

Then we're able, finally, to let go of the past. We release the bound-up energy of our history, and allow that energy to flow into aliveness, into *being*. And we let go of the future, all those projections and fantasies. That doesn't mean that we can't plan for the future, or that we can't remember the past. But our energy is no longer trapped there. Rather, it's right here. *We're* right here.

~

So we find the balance, the place where we're free. Freedom *is* balance. You know this! You already know it—you already *are* it. You don't have to become it. You simply have to find out how to allow that knowing to come to the foreground; and how to allow it to lead you home. That's all.

So you can drop all your ideas about "getting it." There's no getting it—there's just being it. There's no "getting" at all—only giving and receiving. Getting is a kind of acquisition, but there's no acquiring; there's nothing to acquire. There's only relinquishing, and accepting. And that's a relief! Letting go is always a relief.

And in that place of letting go, that realm of compassion, *then* we can truly forgive. When we forgive our own humanity its imperfections, we automatically forgive everyone else as well. Not just mentally or psychologically, but *profoundly*. In that forgiveness, we become free of the burden of all we've been holding, and the heart becomes infinite. Our fellow humans are no longer separate from us, even if we don't know them personally.

When we let go, we stop running, we stop hiding. All that is ended. As I've often said, readiness is when you come to the end of running and hiding. You realize you can't do it anymore; running and hiding no longer work. If they did, you wouldn't be here.

So just be this energy, be this awareness, this aliveness. That's enough. Then everything is as it is—complete.

Returning to Awareness

Holding on is what ego, the protective identity, does. That's its nature—to hold on, to control. To manipulate, protect, defend. But when we find the truth, or when the truth finds us; when we discover the truth, or the truth finds us; when we *directly experience* the truth, we find this emptiness, or vastness, or boundarylessness. This is often defined or explained as infinite consciousness, or the Divine, or Buddha Nature. In that openness, as we become familiar with our true nature, letting go naturally happens.

So it isn't a forced pushing. If there's an effort to let go, then who's efforting? What's the agenda? Where there's an agenda there's an identity. But when we live as consciousness, there's no more identity and no more agenda. There's just awareness, just the mystery. And if, as awareness, we're faced with the movement of emotion, there's no resistance to that movement. So the fear—or anger, or grief, or helplessness—can actually circulate, move, flow, and you begin to understand that emotion is simply energy.

That energy can of course be experienced as intense, painful and scary, and our minds can create a lot of ideas and interpretations based on our emotions. These ideas are usually well-intentioned attempts by ego to stop and protect, to make us safe or secure; but true security is only possible when we let go of the identity that needs to be secure.

Being awareness means there is no one who is being aware. There's no separation between *what is* and the awareness of it. Ego's version of awareness is "me" experiencing "what I'm aware of." That's not what I mean by awareness. That's a certain limited kind of awareness, of course, just as there's a certain limited kind of letting go that's ego-based. All of these descriptions—letting go, feeling, being, and so on—can be co-opted by ego, can be understood from ego's perspective.

But once you've had the truth revealed, even briefly, you can't really put the genie back in the bottle. You can't go backwards. Now the question becomes, how do I finish the job? How do I allow the process of *letting go* to complete itself? Maybe you just remind yourself to keep coming back to awareness. But even that may be too much. "Remind" isn't even the right word, because the awareness that we fundamentally are doesn't live in time. It's not in the past or in the future—past and future are thoughts. It can't be remembered, so there's nothing to be reminded of in the usual way. It's just here, and it's just now. That's all.

So how *do* you find yourself, how can you return to now? That's all you have to discover—how to find yourself right back here. Everything else will reveal itself, everything else will just unfold naturally. You could say you learn to get out of the way of what's happening by being present. Literally *being* present. Then there's no *one* being present, there's just *being* present. There's no one trying to get enlightened. As long as there's someone waiting to get enlightened, it never happens.

Allowing the Struggle

One of the many gifts of being alive is that we get to keep discovering. In a very real sense, there's *only* discovering, only the receiving of our experience, whatever it is in each moment. It's easy to miss that in our rush to get somewhere. If we're looking for something outside ourselves—liberation, for instance—we're focused on the goal, but we might miss the looking. But the looking is what's actually happening, right here, in this moment. So if you can catch yourself in the act of trying to skip to the conclusion, then the compulsion to search for something, to be somewhere else, can drop away, leaving only the realization that you're *already here.*

We often believe that we have to find something we don't have, or change something about ourselves to make things better. And on a practical level that's fine, no problem. Sometimes it's healthy to make adjustments. But from the perspective of simple presence—of being *fully* present, fully alive—there's nothing that needs to be found, or achieved, or fixed, or even understood. You can be human, with all your human imperfections, still learning and growing and maturing, and at the same time fully awake, fully alive.

One of the most limiting beliefs you can have is that spiritual realization requires that you somehow become perfected or sanitized on a human level. But no, you can be exactly as you are. How could you be any other way? Of course, as you deepen in presence, you may find things changing quite dramatically as old patterns and attachments begin to dissolve and fall away; but that happens by itself. It's not something you have to do. It's not your doing. It's not even your business! You'll find yourself surprised by it: "Hm, something's different, something's missing. How'd that happen?"

So you drop the belief that you have to do it, and also the ego trip that you did it. All that is gone. What's happening is just happening—that's all. It's amazing, miraculous, and completely ordinary. Then we get to truly live life, really *live* our life as it is, as it actually is. We get to be *fully* human, completely real. We can truly learn and grow, explore and discover. We can work, create, serve.

So if you find yourself looking, or seeking, or avoiding; grasping at your experience or pushing it away; or experiencing confusion, which is its own sort of struggle with what's present; if you find yourself struggling in any of these ways, stop and tune into your body. Feel the pressure, or the tension, or the anxiety. Feel the emotions that are present—maybe longing, or maybe grief or sadness. Be aware of what's happening in your body, and in your mind.

You don't need to stop it, or fix it, or figure it out. Just allow yourself to become aware of it—that's enough. The thought, "How can I fix this so I can be at peace?" is already a step too far. It's already missing the moment. It's like searching everywhere for your glasses without realizing that you're wearing them. All that's required is just to recognize what's actually here—that's it. And you'll find, as you begin to cultivate awareness—as you begin to live *as* awareness—that when you find yourself back in the struggle, you naturally allow that struggle, allow it to move as it will. As you allow that movement, awareness reemerges, returns to the foreground.

That's what's meant by surrender, and by trust. It's not that we like the struggle, or that it should be pleasant, because it often isn't. But there's a sense of knowing—not an intellectual knowing, but a deep acceptance in one's being—that "this too shall pass," as it were. The struggle is seen as a movement of energy. And when that energy is allowed to move, when that natural process is allowed to complete itself, presence deepens.

This isn't something you can believe or will to happen. Understanding develops naturally as gradually one becomes more aware of presence, of this openness that we are. You find then that it's okay to be identified, okay to be struggling. It's not a problem that needs to be fixed. The condition needs only to be seen or felt or experienced as it is. That is compassion, truly.

And when the struggle drops away and there's peace, what's then experienced is often overwhelming gratitude and love, and a tremendous appreciation of each moment, an amazing enjoyment of even the simplest things. The color of a flower, a passing breeze. Just being here with others, sharing this stillness.

The ego is not going to understand that it's not responsible for this. It's invested in being responsible. And that's fine! Let the ego do what it does, knowing that its attempts to understand, or get it, or figure it out are just what they are—the natural play of that structure, the ego's natural activity. Is that going to change? No. That activity will continue, but you'll cease being identified with it. You'll no longer be doing it. From the perspective of awareness, there's no one doing anything. That's freedom.

Relief Is Only the Beginning

We want to find the way to the end of suffering. So we sit down, and we stop for a bit. We offer ourselves a little stillness, a little silence.

And yet there's still movement. The movement may be pleasurable, or it may be painful. It may be mental, physical, energetic or emotional. Sometimes the movement feels like resistance, pain or struggle, but the natural momentum is always—*always*—toward opening. And as you continue moving into opening, it just gets more amazing; at least that's what I've found.

I think most people who've experienced real depth of awakening would have to admit that they don't really know what it means or where it's going. They can describe their experience to some extent, but ultimately, the nature of what's actually happening remains a mystery. And that's fine! The mind may want the security of some reassuring conceptual understanding, but that's just wanting, another natural movement. Wanting isn't it. *We* are it, actually. We are it. And when we're aligned consciously with that understanding, we feel the pull of the opening, of the expansion, and we allow it.

An often-quoted Zen poem begins, "There's nowhere to go, there's nothing to do." Now, some people misunderstand that. Does that mean we literally don't go anywhere and don't do anything? Maybe, if that happens to be the situation, but not necessarily. "Nowhere to go and nothing to do" is really a description of peace. It's a description of arriving in the moment, and allowing the moment to be whatever it is. It's about allowing the movement and the stillness simultaneously, and *being* the stillness and *being* the movement in the stillness; *being* the light and the expansion of awareness.

Further, it's about having the innocence to allow *not knowing* what this moment is, or what it means. That innocence is very fresh, very light and tender. And it's amazing what keeps arriving in the space of that innocence. The experience is of endless discovery, but entirely without conclusions. In the beginning, one is usually motivated by the desire for relief from suffering, relief from the struggle, relief from the identity with condition. But the relief of freedom is only the beginning of this endless opening.

The Only Thing Holding Us Back

The only thing holding us back from being free is that which we're avoiding. So the solution seems easy—just stop avoiding, right? The problem is that what we're avoiding is often unconscious. So how can it become conscious? How can it be revealed? That's the question.

Interestingly enough, everything we're avoiding is trying to reveal itself all the time. It's either a kind of pressure from within pushing outward, or a gravitational force field drawing us inward. That push, or that pull, is what led people over all these thousands of years to experiment on themselves, and to gradually discover that sitting—quietly, silently—could facilitate actually perceiving the subtle pushing and pulling of what was being avoided. Otherwise those movements might remain unobserved, beneath our notice.

Another way to reveal what's being avoided is to take a look at what you believe. Now, often what we believe is not entirely conscious either, but it's nevertheless running the show. A lot of beliefs stem from very early conditioning. They're really deeply programmed in, and we may not even know we believe them. The best way to identify these unconscious beliefs is to find where the emotional or energetic charge is in your thinking. In other words, notice what arouses your passions, what pushes your buttons. When your unconscious beliefs are challenged, you'll get agitated. Notice that!

I often point people towards emotion as a place to work, because it's a realm that is not fundamentally cognitive. It's more primal, more organic. It arises more directly from the organism, and isn't overlaid with meaning, with belief. It's our beliefs that keep the avoidance unconscious. When an unconscious belief is suddenly, deeply revealed, you may be very surprised by what's under there. It may not be what you think!

Anything that pushes your buttons shows you a great place to start. People on a spiritual path sometimes think, "I shouldn't have my buttons pushed. I shouldn't be reactive anymore. I should be calm." They often then begin repressing emotion, and think they're becoming free of reactivity. But what they're really doing is burying it deeper. That doesn't work! That energy will still manifest somehow, whether as some kind of health problem or through compulsive acting out.

And that's the other thing that doesn't work: acting out. You can try it as much as you like and, of course, we all do. And then maybe we beat ourselves up a bit for it, beat our heads against that particular wall for a while. Eventually, though, we find out that beating ourselves up doesn't work either, and we find ourselves back where we started, right here with whatever is moving.

We're always faced with this challenge, the process of finding the balance between instinct and clarity. We begin to see the instinctual drives of our human organism and learn to allow them, to accept them. Anger arises? That's okay. It's okay to be angry. Actually, the description "It's okay to be angry" doesn't quite capture what I'm really saying, because it seems to imply being *someone* who is angry. But to truly allow anger is the end of that someone—and often the end of the anger as well! The key is simply allowing the movement of that energy, and dropping the identification with what's happening.

When that identity drops, the truth is self-evident; the presence that we are becomes obvious. From that perspective, our humanity is just what it is: up and down, light and heavy, joyful and angry—the whole range of human experience. The stillness, the vastness of awareness, includes all of it, and we are that.

Vastness is not an identity; it's actually nothing at all. But language is limited when we're talking about the infinite. And there's still this human life, and this human body we find ourselves living in. It's endlessly challenging for most people, learning how to take care of this body, this life, that we've been given. But what an amazing gift it is nevertheless. Sometimes it's almost too much, isn't it?

So to come full circle, what we're avoiding is actually what we want. That which we're running from is actually that which we're yearning for. The way to freedom from what we're avoiding lies in opening to that pushing and pulling, that resistance, and not naming it; not identifying with it; not fixing it, or controlling it, or categorizing it, or believing it, or rejecting it. You've probably heard it said that there's nothing to do, and no one to do it; that it's already done. This is what that means. Simply be the awareness that encompasses it and permeates all of it. Everything becomes radiant. Everything is radiance itself.

And then we find that we're guided in all kinds of odd and unexpected ways. We're faced with all kinds of situations in our lives, and often our path is unclear. But then we receive a kind of guidance that's mysterious and surprising, and not at all what we expect! So the willingness to be surprised is really useful. That's why one of my favorite things is to be wrong. I love being wrong! It's really amusing. And being wrong is a good thing to be amused by, because if your identity is wrapped up in being right, then trust me, you're going to suffer a lot.

Needing to be right is about belief—about, once again, beliefs we don't even know we have. Beliefs make the mind brittle, and fragile. But when you start questioning deeply, your mind begins to soften, and gradually becomes malleable like damp clay. Questioning is the moisture that softens that hardness, that relaxes that rigidity. You want your mind to be malleable, it's very important. Otherwise you'll find yourself rigidly adhering to positions. Being flexible is much more fun.

Questioning often releases a lot of energy. It might be scary, particularly as you approach your most deeply held beliefs. But fear, fundamentally, is just energy. So is anger. So is grief. They're natural expressions of our vitality, our life force. That's what feeling is—it's the passion of life. And it's the very fuel that we need, that we can use to become liberated from the identity, from the belief in "me." It's the fuel, the fire, the shakti. We are all shakti. Everything is. Realization is simply shifting into that awareness, that understanding. That's all. It's already happening. The sun is already radiating. We *are* the sun. We really are.

Reality Begins When the Story Ends

It's so beautiful when the story stops. By "the story" I mean the internal monologue by which we explain to ourselves what we think is happening, or what's going to happen, or what did happen. We've all had moments when the mind gets out of the way, and we're suddenly no longer separated from reality by our descriptions of it. We all know that openness of being, if we're willing to recognize it.

But it's not necessary to stop the story intentionally; as I'm sure you've noticed, that doesn't work! In fact it's fine to tell yourself stories. Creating stories is what the mind does, that's its function. And our minds enjoy stories! They're fiction, and we love fiction. We love taking it in, and we love creating it. We may sometimes get confused and think our stories are reality, but they're not. Our descriptions of reality are just that—descriptions. Reality itself is unspeakable and unknowable.

As long as you remember that a story is just a story, then you don't have to believe it. You can be surprised by it, or entertained by it. You can react to it, and experience how it affects you emotionally. But gradually you come to see clearly that you in your essence are not the story. You are the awareness that precedes the story. That awareness—that which you truly are—is reality. In that realization is freedom.

Don't avoid insecurity; embrace it.
That's where the doorway to the heart opens.

Be grateful for delicate, vulnerable insecurity.

Readiness

If you're looking for it, it can't be seen. If you're listening for it, it can't be heard. If you're sensing for it, it can't be felt. So how is it possible to truly perceive reality? It's possible only if you're ready.

But what is readiness? Can you *get* ready? In some sense, all of the practices and techniques developed and taught over the millennia are about "getting ready," about purifying the body, mind and heart so that one can really be available to this moment. So that one can listen without listening—without *being* a listener—or see without looking, sense without sensing. So one can simply *be here* without trying.

But can you *really* do anything to get ready? Who knows? Some people think you can. Some of them have been working on it for a long time! When I was a Zen monk, I used to sit sesshin—eighteen hours a day on a zafu with my legs crossed. It was a lot of effort. I'm sure it was valuable. Sometimes people put in long years of that kind of effort, but when they eventually come to a place of simple presence, they look back and say that all that effort wasn't necessary. But actually, they did go through it, didn't they? How do they know it wasn't necessary?

The truth is, what's actually necessary is exactly what we go through. Whether you're doing practices, purification, therapy, whatever, each of us finds our own way. Can you find someone else's way? I don't think so! Nor can you copy someone else's way. You can try—lots of people do!—but you'll end up frustrated.

It's important to understand that you can find your own way. Then you can begin to have confidence in the deep truth that's leading you. Otherwise you're always comparing and contrasting yourself with what other people are doing. That's disempowering, and energetically draining. You need energy for this path—energy, focus and grounding.

But whatever you go through on your way there, readiness appears when you're done hiding and you're done running. Hiding and running don't work any more. You've seen through that game. You know you can't escape. As long as you still think you can escape, you're not ready, at least not in that moment. But maybe the next moment! It really isn't about developing along a timeline that goes from past to future—it's *right now.* Readiness is *only* now. That simplifies things, doesn't it? It's right here. You don't have to get somewhere else.

But if you do feel like you still need to get somewhere else, then that's where you're at. That's not a problem! There's a bit of fog over the sun obscuring the light, dimming the brightness. A lot of things obscure reality. Unfelt emotion, for instance, can be held in the body as tension or fear, creating blockages. So we allow ourselves to become intimate with our condition, whatever that condition happens to be in this moment. Whether we like it or dislike it, or we want it to be different, or think it *should* be different—whatever our feelings about our condition, we nevertheless allow it to be what it actually is, and to do what it actually does. Then, as the old saying goes, "The snake sheds its skin when it's ready."

So when you find that you're finally finished with trying to get somewhere else, then suddenly you find yourself *right here.* You may not like it, exactly; it may be painful, it may be very difficult. But when you're ready, you're through telling yourself how it should be. That strategy doesn't work any more; that story no longer holds your interest. Rather, you're simply available to this moment, whatever it offers—the feelings, the energies, the sensations; the revelations, the openings, the vulnerability.

So can you allow yourself to be here, fully and completely? Not off in a thought or concept called "being here," but really, simply *here.* Dropping ideas about it, dropping body and mind. What's left? *This.* Everything. Love, connection, oneness. All the good stuff that we used to want, and that we now realize we *are*.

The amazing thing is that when you come to an environment like satsang where there is a focus on presence, on aliveness, just being in this space is deeply beneficial. The environment that we create by being together in this way is literally a transformative field. Do we understand it? Can we figure it out? Not really. I'm not saying this to offer you something to believe, but more to encourage you to be open to surrendering and finding out for yourself.

So is there anything in you that's still trying right now? Is there anything that's still struggling, right now, in your body or in your mind? Is there any attempt to get away from this moment? If there is you'll know it. It may make you uncomfortable; you may have ideas about that, or judgments. Or you may find yourself just deepening into silence, into spaciousness, into open-heartedness.

Surrender isn't about having a certain experience. It's about simple, open availability to whatever *is*, right now.

The Role of the Mind

What is the point of talking about the inexpressible? Since reality can't be defined, explained or understood by the analytical mind, why bother?

The thinking mind, as much trouble as it can be, is also a function of the inexpressible and clearly has an agenda of wanting to know and understand. The sooner we can acknowledge its positive intent, the sooner it becomes our ally on the journey into the unknown. When the mind becomes our ally, it becomes supportive and caring, compassionate and patient. And useful! A relaxed, smoothly functioning mind is an amazing tool to have at one's disposal.

This is important, because for the so-called vast heart to open, the mind has to be basically at peace; from a simple physics point of view, it can't be using up all the energy in the system. Otherwise, by trying to create meaning the mind actually contracts into a defensive posture, consuming energy that would otherwise naturally expand into radiant vastness.

The ongoing process of integrating the mind with the body and heart is best described as *energy management*. We learn to manage ourselves energetically so that the mind can relax, allow what is, and assume its natural role as our ally rather than our protector.

The tendency to look for the "right signs" to reassure us that we are doing well on the spiritual path is actually an example of the thinking mind getting in the way, attempting to protect us by controlling our trajectory along the path, keeping us "on track" by following an identified set of guideposts.

As the mind learns to relax its defenses, however, the whole dynamic shifts. As our ally, the mind drops its attempts at controlling, and the mystery is allowed to unfold itself. We realize that to simply recognize what is, without attempting to control it in any way, is the true doorway to freedom.

~

The thinking mind really can be a powerful ally, and we need all the friends we can get! The path can sometimes be lonely, and if we're challenging ourselves, or judging ourselves, or doubting ourselves—things the mind so often does—that can make it much harder.

It's really about redirecting energy. You don't have to control or fight the mind—that doesn't work. Simply allow the mind to do what it does, and be willing to express the truth of whatever condition arises. In that expression, you facilitate the path. When a condition is up for you, some human condition that's irritating or agitating or difficult or upsetting, simply express it into openness. Often something then immediately releases, and you're back in spaciousness and freedom.

The value of this kind of expression is simply *that it works.* So let it work. Let your expression be *just expression.* You're not expressing to get something or to produce a particular outcome. You're not trying to understand, or fix something, or figure anything out. It's simply and only expression. Expression is part of our human beauty, whether it's poetry or a description of suffering. It's okay to be human, okay to express even our nasty or embarrassing conditions, the many ways we don't live up to our own or others' expectations about how we're supposed to be.

So expression doesn't have to interfere with deepening into the vastness of the unknown. On the contrary, it can very much facilitate it. If you've ever done journaling, you may have found that from time to time there's a sudden opening, and something just comes out that needed to be communicated. And sometimes the conditioned needs to be not only communicated, but also heard in openness, witnessed in a non-judgmental, completely accepting space of listening.

The mind, ultimately, is neutral. It's a thinking machine. But it sometimes gets infused with passion, and things get more complicated. That's why Joe Miller, that wonderful Sufi teacher, used to say, "You can get more stinkin' from thinkin' than you can from drinkin'—but to feel is for real." When the thinking is experienced as suffering, then there's the fire of feeling, the energy of feeling, happening as well. So turn towards that feeling. Give it your attention. Sit with it. Or express it! Whatever works. That's what you get to find out in every moment—what works.

So invite your thinking mind to be an ally, and see what happens. The truth is constantly revealing itself, and it's always showing us the way. Our true nature is always here waiting for us to pay attention. Finding out how to listen to that—*that's* the key to the inner path to truth and freedom. Everyone has that. It's our nature. It's not something you have to attain, or get from outside yourself. You might have to learn how to recognize it, how to allow it to function.

So we just keep learning. I think that's really life's function—constant learning and growth and transformation. Everything is a miracle. If you stop for a moment, just stop and take it all in, this life is mind-blowing. Completely, incredibly, impossibly mind-blowing. Isn't it?

The Light of Attention

One of my favorite places to walk is a particular beach at Bolinas. It's covered with what must be billions of rocks, but if you look carefully, you find little treasures. One of the things I like to look for there is abalone shell. There are usually just fragments, because the seals crack open the live abalone and eat them, but those little fragments are like jewels among the rocks. The thing I love about abalone is that depending on how the light hits it, you see turquoise or purple, different greens, different pinks—it's amazing. Even if it's just sitting on a shelf during the day, as the sun changes, the colors keep changing. It's like a magical jewel. And this really offers a perfect metaphor for how, depending on the kind of light we shine on our experience, we see things differently.

If we're able to do that effectively—if we can shine the light of our attention in a way that allows us to open to what is, to allow what is—then we become, in a sense, one with reality. Our experience becomes very direct, and is no longer filtered by our ideas, beliefs or conclusions about what's happening. We return to the truth of who we truly are, of our fundamental nature, which is prior to all that. We return to the simple reality of aliveness, of vitality. And then we just do whatever we do. We enjoy our lives, and live them fully.

It's not about living up to some ideal, or being "spiritual" in some contrived way. It's about *actually awakening,* and cultivating that awakening in each moment. And if what we find in the moment is resistance or struggle, confusion or frustration, then it's important to question our attitude, how we're relating to what's happening. What kind of light are we shining on our experience? We may need to unravel the mental grip, the mental defense mechanism, so we can free up the energy of what's being held in emotionally—old pain, grief or fear—so that it can move without being restricted by whatever ideas or meaning the mind attaches to it.

As I've often recommended, think of this process as *energy management*. You start wherever you are, and bring attention to what needs attention, and gradually what's been held begins to move. Slowly the stuckness dissolves, and your energy flows freely. You become fluid movement, and awakening, your true condition, is naturally revealed.

Awakening is not accomplished, not created. You don't need to believe in it. You don't need to understand it. And not needing to understand is a great relief! Socrates said, "The only true wisdom is in knowing that you know nothing." If you can accept the gift of *not knowing*, then everything is new. Everything is amazing.

Everyone Is the Teacher

When we're open, we're sensitized to the intimacy of the shared presence of our being, and satsang becomes a miraculous environment. It's kind of like a spiritual greenhouse. The added light and warmth encourages growth, facilitates rooting and bourgeoning. The resonance of consciousness engenders itself. And then we talk about what's happening, we describe how the movement feels *right now*. We expose what needs to be exposed. On the surface, it may look like a question and answer session, but it's really much more far out than that. When someone comes up to speak, it's really all of us up here. In reality there isn't even any "up here" or "over there." That's just how it looks on the surface.

Whether or not you come up and speak, simply listening is powerful, and also not separate from what's happening at the front of the room. If someone describes a condition that's difficult, they may experience some heaviness, or pain, or grief, or fear. If they allow themselves to really merge into the experience instead of remaining separate from it, then in that instant opening begins to happen, and the whole room expands. Even though the person may still be experiencing their pain very vividly, the room continues expanding. In that expansion, the listening is very powerful.

In satsang, there's an energetic maturing of the environment that happens quite naturally. It's not something we're doing, but rather our allowing of the space simply to unfold as it is. And because everyone is "it," everyone is the teacher. Everyone is the dharma, the energy, the transformation of being into consciousness. We drop these limited identities of student and teacher. They may initially be useful in a limited way, but ultimately they really don't mean anything.

Here in this moment, dialog is almost irrelevant. Dialog is fine, of course, but the real key is simply allowing listening in this space, letting what happens happen. And it *does* happen, whether or not there's verbal interaction. Everything we think and feel is simply energy. When we become that energy consciously, nothing can be stuck anymore. Not for long, anyway; maintaining stuckness becomes too difficult.

Being Available to What Is

Our dialog is not an intellectual pursuit. Dialog here is a vehicle for letting go into our true nature. That's its only purpose. It's not an attempt to construct a system of thought or belief—opening to our true nature deconstructs belief. But if you're still struggling or holding on to something, that's fine, we can still have a dialog. Wherever you are is fine—it's the only place you *can* be! That may seem rather simple, but actually, if you really get that, it may be the only thing you need to get.

~

Q. How did you know when you were finally, truly, free? And when that happened, did you feel like you were done?

There is no concept about it. There is no identity about it.

Q. Then what is the secret to tasting freedom? I sit almost every day, and I try not to try, or expect, or think, or do anything. But I just can't seem to get that taste of freedom I've heard about that would give me a sense of the direction of truth.

The problem is you're still trying. You're looking for an experience that you've heard about or read about. That's the danger of hearing about and reading about the truth—you end up with a lot of distracting ideas and preconceptions. So instead, I would invite you simply to feel exactly what you're feeling, simply to sense exactly what you're sensing, right now—and then drop the "I" that's perceiving it. Simply be that awareness.

Whatever is present right now, even if it's something painful—*that* is the doorway. And that doorway will open by itself. Ego can try to open it, but ego, even in the act of trying to be open, is actually holding on. So by being in the body or relaxing, maybe feeling the breath or resting your feet on the ground, you can simply allow what is without looking for what isn't; without looking for the experience of so-called awakening. Because awakening is fundamentally what we are, it can't be achieved or even found. It can only reveal itself.

So all that's required is to be available to *what is* in this moment. If there's an idea present about what you're hoping to experience, that idea may be obscuring what you're actually sensing. Maybe there's some feeling coming up that you don't want to feel; often we avoid feeling. But feeling, when we drop into the direct experience of it, is energy. It's not conceptual. Mostly when people block feeling, it's because that feeling hurts, and because they have ideas about what the feeling means or says about them. "Only weak people cry," or "Spiritually-evolved people don't get angry." These constructs are all defense mechanisms we've developed to avoid feeling pain.

But when you realize that feeling is not conceptual—that it's energy—then you simply surrender to that movement. And when the movement has been allowed to happen, what's left is openness, spaciousness, which is awakened consciousness. It's boundless! And as you taste that—and maybe you have tasted that, or had a glimpse of it—then, understandably, you want more. But of course, trying to get more only pushes the awareness of it away. That's why it's been said that every step towards it is a step away from it.

So you learn simply to be present. At first you think if you're not feeling that openness you must not be getting it, or you must be doing the wrong thing; this must be the wrong path, or the wrong teacher. Or you're just not worthy, or it's the wrong lifetime. We draw so many conclusions! The key is to avoid getting caught by the conclusions, and instead question all of them: are they true?

So cultivate questioning. True questioning leads to *not knowing*, the source of real wisdom. Observe what you are concluding, and ask yourself: do I really know this to be true? By cultivating questioning you create the possibility for the defense mechanisms of the mental process to unravel, and gradually you learn to live in *not knowing*, which is *being understanding*, or awakened consciousness. It can be scary to admit that you don't know, but that fear may itself be the doorway. Whatever the doorway is for you will always be present. Always! For everyone, at every moment. That's just the way it is.

~

Q. What do you mean by "the doorway"?

The doorway is the entry point into the awareness of our true nature, and that doorway can manifest in an infinite number of ways. Generally speaking, the doorway appears as some kind of resistance, some kind of ego-protective mechanism. The ego is actually very well-intentioned—its purpose is simply to protect the human organism. It's our identity with ego that leads to resistance, contraction and suffering. When we've awakened to our true nature, however, we see ego for what it is, and we cease being identified with it. Ego is then simply a functional aspect of our humanity, and not fundamentally a problem.

Q. When I'm available to what I'm resisting, sometimes it does become a doorway. But sometimes I don't appear to be able to come out of resistance around it.

Okay, so there's just resistance, then. Can you be the space of awareness that perceives that resistance?

Q. Sometimes.

Then just be the resistance itself! Don't worry so much about the resistance being a doorway; that idea could itself become an impediment, another limiting concept.

Q. It feels like thinking happens a lot in my meditations. It seems like I just can't turn the thinking off. Can I use the thinking as a doorway, or is it easier just to go into the body and the feelings?

Generally if you attempt to stop the thinking, that's just going to be a struggle, a holding on, that creates more contraction. Fortunately, you don't have to stop the thinking; just let the thinking think. The mental realm just does what it does—let it. And instead of putting your energy and attention into thinking, redirect it into sensing. Don't fight against thinking, or try to force thinking to stop; just gently redirect your attention into sensing, breathing, resting.

Thoughts will still arise, but you just don't get involved in them. Just as importantly, you also don't try to push them away. Any attempt at manipulation is a kind of control, and that's what obscures the truth, always. When your energy is no longer going into the thinking mind, it will gradually quiet by itself. Eventually the mind just gives up.

Falling Into the Fire

One of the central questions of the spiritual process is how to allow awareness without getting in the way, without coming from conditioning or from an attempt to manipulate experience. From the perspective of the ego, non-doing is a frightening strategy. The ego is afraid that if no effort is exerted, nothing is going to happen, that it's going to remain mired in stuckness. So you have to be willing to allow that insecurity, that fear that awakening may *not* happen for you, that you may remain in struggle. At some point you find you're willing to let go and fall into the fire of that fear, and in that surrender you find that light appears in the darkness. As Rumi says, you go through the fire and you end up in the water. But until you take that leap you don't find out.

Often, though, people do "find out" for a time, but then find themselves caught back in the condition again and think they've done something wrong. But they haven't done anything wrong; that's just how the process works. From our subjective perspective we don't necessarily see the larger picture—that our awareness is expanding. We may glimpse it at times, when we experience breakthroughs or large integrations, but more often people aren't even aware that they are "progressing spiritually," so to speak. This is where trust becomes important—trust in the integrity of our own process.

As you bring awareness to the struggle—to the resistance to what is, or to the wanting to change it—and learn to really allow that struggle, then all of a sudden there can come a moment of freedom. Maybe just a glimpse, maybe just a taste, but with that taste you know, in a way you never have before, that freedom is truly possible. That's why Suzuki-roshi said that practice *begins* with enlightenment. Awakening, the discovery or recognition of your true nature, is the real beginning. And as Krishnamurti said, it's the truth that sets us free, not our effort to be free.

So when truth appears, give truth your attention. And when it's not there, have compassion for the human condition. Compassion means recognizing that our humanness is what it is, and allowing it to be that. Emotion may arise—fear, grief, maybe anger. If people don't know how to let the emotion move, they'll either repress or act out, creating all kinds of mental fixations. The spiritual process is an energetic unraveling, so as I've often said, navigating that process is really about learning appropriate *energy management*.

I've often used the analogy of placing an ice cube in a bowl of warm water. The ice cube melts away, and then there's only water; the ice and the warm water are the same substance. Similarly, the essence of the limited condition is truth; ultimately, truth is all there is. So *everything* must be allowed to exist. Otherwise we become fractured, internally divided. It can be tempting to deny aspects of our experience that don't seem "spiritual" enough, but those experiences, which we sometimes call "suffering," are really just patterns of energy. As you realize that the self *is* fundamentally energy, everything begins to return to the source.

The various temporary forms the energy takes—the physical body, the mind, the personality, and so on—are useful, functional, creative, but ultimately impermanent. It's the life that animates them that is the infinite mystery. The only way to really, fully allow that life is to begin to let yourself experience how it works, little by little.

Even one tiny experience is like a seed. You let that seed fall and take root and pretty soon, if the ground is fertile, it sprouts. You begin to distinguish between the effort that's ego-based and the "effort" that really isn't effort. That second kind of effort is difficult to talk about until you're a little more established in presence, in truth. What I'm saying may or may not seem to make sense depending on where you're at.

I like to use the image of the sun radiating light. You become the sun, in a way. But it's not like, "Hey, I'm the sun!" There's no identity involved. There's no one who says, "Hey, I'm really spiritual now. I'm really getting this enlightenment thing!" No, thank you. That's not it. That's what's called "the stink of Zen," the inflated *identity* of being spiritual. That may arise temporarily, as a kind of crutch to get you past a certain point; but it's no more real than any other kind of identity, and eventually it falls away.

Crutches are fine, actually; they can be useful, temporarily. Many people utilize spiritual technologies like meditation, for instance, and if they are understood and used well they can be very helpful. The same can be true of satsang. Many people first experience truth in a satsang environment. They often then associate truth with being in satsang, so they start coming every week to get that "satsang high." And that's okay! That's fine for a while. But at some point, if you're really committed, you have to see through that delusion.

It's important not to think of Truth as a state to achieve, as if by having enough "high" experiences you'll somehow become permanently high. It's important to understand that freedom is not a state that can be created or held on to. Because freedom is already what we are, we can never lose it. The fact that you're not conscious of truth doesn't mean that it's not fully present already, but only that it hasn't yet revealed itself in your conscious experience. That's the only difference. You are already 100% free. You are already 100% enlightened. But that may not be evident from your individual perspective. Why? Because the ego's attempts at self-protection are in the way. The identity of ego is foreground.

So simply become aware of ego, and gradually it will dissolve. It's not about cultivating a particular state or condition, it's about seeing the truth. Not some concept called "The Truth," but the direct experience of that which concepts can only point to. Of course teachings or beliefs can sometimes be helpful in inspiring you to hang in there through the difficult times, when it's really rough. Our human lives are often very difficult. But freedom is ultimately the end of beliefs, the end of adhering to concepts about what is. As you come to understand that, your concepts begin to unravel.

That's a great way to become insecure! I don't mean becoming insecure in the sense of giving yourself a hard time on purpose; I mean letting go of your habitual strategies for creating security, just enough so that some movement can begin to happen; so that the movement of being can come to the foreground. Find out how to let that happen. That's really what it's about, finding out how to let the truth come forward.

That's why coming to satsang is helpful. If you feel it here, great, it's in the foreground. Let it be! All you have to do is enjoy it. Love it. Let it fill you. Let it fill everything. Let it fill the pain, the suffering, the confusion. Let it fill whatever is present. As we allow that here in a group setting, it facilitates everyone's transformation. You feel the consciousness in the room expanding. It just happens.

Obsession

The obsessive mind is addictive. It has a life of its own. It cannot be controlled or manipulated, and ultimately it cannot be satisfied. Consider, for example, the longing one might experience in unrequited love. Many thoughts and feelings might arise about the desired person, but underneath would always be the essential pain of longing.

Longing is its own reality. Its nature, literally, is *not getting the unavailable.* It isn't about being satisfied. Its reality is *being unsatisfied.* In the immortal words of Mick Jagger, "I can't get no satisfaction"! If one remains caught in trying to get satisfaction, the obsessive mind continues to be fueled by that desire.

So how do we become free of the obsessive mind? By letting the intense energy of the underlying emotional state fully discharge through the body. This can only happen when we give 100% of our attention to *what is*—in this case, the movement of the emotion, or the pain of longing. This attention does not arise from personal will, but from the absence of a self. This 100% attention is pure awareness: it is without story or projection, without anticipation or expectation, without conclusions or judgments. It is pure intelligence, and pure wisdom.

If a particular obsessive pattern is very old, arising from early conditioning or early wounding, then it may recur, even as we deepen into awareness. One may naturally be concerned about—or disturbed by—this recurrence. But in reality, the pattern's recurrence is not our problem, or even our business. We simply need to ride the waves when they arise. At some point, the pattern becomes fully dissolved into awareness. We cannot know when this will happen or how long it will take.

So in our example of longing: when the longing has been

fully allowed, but not acted upon, a clarity opens in our heart, and we find ourselves free of the obsessive mind. The vastness of our true heart has blossomed, and the fragrance of its essential nature, love, fills every realm of perception.

Tending To This Moment

Sitting around doing nothing doesn't mean nothing gets done. Indeed, you could say that when energy is moving, something *is* getting done—even though there might not be anyone doing it! So we come here to sit, to cultivate and hopefully to realize our true nature, which is awakened presence, awakened consciousness, awakened energy.

I'd like to talk a little about how we approach the doer, that part of our self that's trying, that's pushing, and that's also resisting. We can't really drop the doer through any effort of our own. What we can do, however, is notice the quality of how we relate to our practice. What I'd like to suggest is that instead of being a practitioner—instead of approaching practice from the position of someone who is practicing—instead, try out being an attendant. So rather than trying or doing something in this moment, you're simply *tending to* this moment. You're taking care of this moment. You're following this moment, rather than leading it.

Tending to is not controlling. Rather, it is surrender, submission. That doesn't mean it lacks energy or focus or clarity or strength; but its strength is not the strength of aggressive will. It's the strength of patience, and the courage to really listen. There's a freedom, an effortlessness in being an attendant. You're just taking care of what needs to be taken care of.

As we sit silently like this, moment to moment, you may begin noticing very subtle energies, tensions, movements, vibrations, emotions, thoughts, distractions, sounds. In the richness of this moment, are you *trying* to be present? Or are you simply *tending to* what's being given, to what's coming in? It's really just a subtle shift in attention or attitude. Suzuki-roshi said "Attitude is everything." I think that's what he meant—the quality of our attention.

Attention is essential, obviously, absolutely essential for awakening, and for liberation. That's why most of the classical teachings include the practice of stillness, physical stillness—not rigid, controlled stillness, but relaxed, open stillness—as a prerequisite for transformation. In stillness the energy can really begin to channel and move, and gradually it can dissolve the blocks in the system.

Attending to your own experience will show you the way. The feedback comes completely naturally. If you're in the way—that is, if you're trying—then you'll experience a contraction, a compression, a holding back. If not, you'll experience opening and expansion instead.

Once you've had a glimpse of truth or awakening, then you follow *that*, really let *that* guide you. In the meantime, you find out how to take care of your life, how to meet each moment as it is presented. That's where tenderness and compassion can begin to be cultivated. In that cultivation, energy moves, and opens, and expands, and deepens, and radiates light.

Another way to think about it is *taking care* of each moment. Maybe the question to ask yourself is "How am I taking care of this moment?" This kind of questioning can be a useful way to shift your attitude, to open up the possibility of another perspective. Flexibility of perspective is very important—don't let yourself be locked into rigidly following one way. That's the doer thinking. The doer always thinks it has "the way." And it can be very convincing.

But that's not it! The way is not convincing. There's nothing to be convinced of, nothing to be proven. The truth is self-evident; it's obvious. If it's not obvious, there's something else present: confusion, fear, longing, sleepiness, distractedness, compulsivity. So we start wherever we are, whatever is present, and we begin to tend.

You'll see that it works, and you'll know when it works, because you'll start to open. You'll begin to be comfortable with nothing. You'll begin to allow yourself ease, and openness, and vulnerability. And as you move through that vulnerability, you'll understand that what we're looking for is really that intimacy, that connection—we have a deep longing for connection with others, and with ourselves.

As we become aware in this way, we see that *tending to* is really just opening to *that*. *That's* what we really surrender to. That's what is meant by being held in the heart of the divine. And then we're really taken care of, profoundly. We find our way, whatever it is in this life. Each one of us has our own journey that we're on.

The Mind Is the Last to Get It

Some people believe that if they meditate hard enough or long enough, or get zapped with enough shakti in satsang, that at some particular moment they'll be instantly trajected into liberated consciousness. Others believe awakening is an ongoing process, a gradual development over time. So I'd like to talk a little bit about this process of transformation—the alchemical process that we're all involved in, one way or another.

Generally when we're learning, we pass through four stages. In the beginning, we're unconsciously incompetent—we don't know that we don't know. In the second stage, we're consciously incompetent—we become aware that there's something we don't know, so we set out to learn it. As we learn, we enter the third stage, becoming consciously competent—we've learned something, and we're self-consciously aware of our new knowledge. And finally there's the fourth stage, when we become unconsciously competent—the knowledge has sunk in to the point where, on a conscious level, we no longer need to be aware of it. The learning has become integrated. That's where many people get confused on the spiritual path. They've had an awakening, or a big opening, and maybe things are different for a while. But then at some point it seems like ordinary reality again—the same old patterns are kicking in—and here people sometimes get discouraged. But what they don't realize is that they've evolved, and are really in a very different place. They've opened and are moving in a bigger field, but they don't see it, because the change has been integrated and is no longer consciously experienced.

This is one of the reasons why the path is not so easy—how can you trust what you don't consciously experience? There are those moments when you think, "I have it now! This is it!" Then reality hits you in the head, and you go into doubt. But doubt points us to the very essence of the process, our fundamental *not knowing*. And gradually we learn to allow ourselves not to know, to relax into that *not knowing*. And we begin to realize that the mind, the mental faculty, as wonderful and interesting as it is, is really the last to get it.

Now some people—maybe most people!—would prefer that the mind be be the *first* to get it; but no, the mind is necessarily the last to get it. And it's always very surprised. It's like, "Huh, I think something is different. Something's absent. I wonder what happened?" It's really very funny, actually. There's a very real sense in which the mind *never* gets it. And that's fine! It's not the mind's job to get it. That's not the mind's function.

P. D. Ouspensky, a student of the Russian mystic G.I. Gurdjieff, wrote that most people don't really have new experiences, because they're always filtering present experience through their old ways of thinking, through sets of preexisting concepts, never perceiving reality directly. But there's a simple antidote to that: feel.

Try it out. Just feel. Sense. Open to the senses: seeing, hearing, smelling, tasting, touching. Breathing! Touching is sensing is feeling. And then here we are, back in this whole moment, this infinite space of presence, of Big Heart. Even if the heart is heavy. The Big Heart can receive anything the emotional heart experiences.

~

Q. You mentioned evolution. Do you think liberation, or seeing our true nature, or the universe seeing itself, or whatever you want to call it—is that the culmination of an evolutionary movement?

No. Liberation is already done. That's where the mind gets confused. That's why I mentioned the argument about instant vs. gradual enlightenment—it's really not so much a disagreement as a confusion. That which we seek is already that which we are; there's no doubt about that. But it isn't quite so simple as that, because if it were, everyone would experience themselves as fully, consciously realized, right?

So the "evolution" that takes place is the dissolving of the ego's reality, the dissolving of the belief that the ego is who you are. That's the transformation—the shift of attention from contracted, defended reality to liberated, infinite consciousness. That's the evolution. In essence it's already done—it's not something that's created or achieved, it's already what we are. Period. It can't be held on to; how could it be?

Q. So the evolution is the breaking down of the ego?

Not so much the breaking down of as the dis-identifying with. Part of the basic condition of the human body-mind is a certain protective contraction that creates a personality. The human need to survive creates the ego structure. That's just part of being human, and it's not a problem. The ego doesn't need to be dismantled, only seen for what it is.

What I'm talking about is a fundamental shift of identity. Teachers of Advaita often recommend the inquiry, "Who am I?" Or, who is it that's asking the question? Who is it that's suffering? Who is it that gets enlightened? To the conceptual mind it's a paradox, but experienced directly it makes perfect sense. You know who you are, but not from the perspective of your thinking mind. You know who you are by the resting of consciousness in itself. You're quite familiar with that, even if you don't consciously know you are. It's truly already done.

Expose the condition completely
in the space of awareness.

That's what honesty really means.

Telling It Like It Is

One of the most important elements in personal transformation is honesty—telling it like it is, however it is. Whether you like it, or you don't like it, or you're pissed off about it. Whether you're terrified, angry, disappointed, frustrated, anxious, confused—whatever. None of that is who you are. When we really speak our truth, it's not personal; it's just what's being experienced, that's all, even if it feels shameful or embarrassing, or whatever judgment we have about it. To acknowledge where we actually are from the perspective of truth, from the perspective of a listening that has no agenda or boundaries and that draws no conclusions, truly sets us free.

When our limited truth is expressed and heard in the space of complete listening, it loses its power to control us. That's how transformation happens.

~

Q. I'm feeling worn out. I watch myself, I watch my judgments and reactions, and I guess I'm feeling impatient with my progress. When I'm by myself reading some cool spiritual book it all sounds really great, but when I'm faced with real situations I just go right back into reactivity.

Be that impatience you feel. That's the answer.

Q. So as I'm feeling impatient, try not to push it away?

That's right. The pushing it away is based on some concept, like "I have to be spiritual like in that cool book," or like this or that teacher said, or whatever. Right?

Q. It's more that I want that experience.

That's what I meant. You want what you don't have. Bingo! That's the key: wanting what you don't have. If you can open to that *wanting*, you will be free. But what happens instead is that becomes a blind spot. The hardest thing for the conscious mind to experience is the unconscious drive. We'll let ourselves see the resistance at the next level up, but we miss the *primary* resistance. And that's what you're expressing now—the primary resistance.

Q. I think I get that. But now I'm finding that my mind is trying to figure it out.

That's part of the dynamic. So notice that, be aware of the whole gestalt, the whole dynamic of figuring it out. Don't put energy into figuring it out, but don't suppress that impulse either. Just let the mind do what it does. As soon as you're aware that you're trying to figure it out, you're no longer caught by that dynamic. A subtle shift has taken place—now you're the awareness that perceives the condition. You're not caught anymore. You can choose to be that awareness.

So you become more intimate with this whole dynamic. And as it happens, you are becoming more present. Which may be uncomfortable! When we encounter pain, our natural instinctual reaction is to withdraw from it. We don't want pain, we want comfort. But ironically, as you remain open and move into greater intimacy with the pain, you become more expanded. You may not see that right now, but it's very evident.

Q. I feel like I'm hitting a wall.

Be the wall. Welcome the wall. Welcome whatever *is* right now.

~

Q. When you've gone through something difficult and you've come out the other side, and you have a lot of fear about that situation recurring, how do you work with that?

Allow yourself to feel the fear that it will happen again.

Q. It's hard to trust again after something like that. You worry all the time.

Again, just allow the fear. You're either allowing it or resisting it, and in fact the statement "It's hard to trust" is an expression of resisting it. So again, can you just allow that fear to be felt? Can you simply feel it now, and not get caught in that imaginary projection of the mind called "the future"?

Even if your prediction was true, even if your bad experience was definitely going to happen again, that still wouldn't matter now, in *this* moment. Here and now, there's still just the fear. People think if they figure out the future they're somehow not going to have to go through what's coming up in the present. But that's not how it works.

As you face powerful challenges like this, you'll begin to experience true learning. Not intellectual learning, but the entrainment of the whole with the vastness of our nervous system; not just the limited bodily nervous system, but the larger, energetic nervous system that's connected to everything and everyone. In the face of this, fear naturally arises, and that fear can become the doorway. Do you want to avoid the doorway?

Q. It's a natural reaction, to avoid the doorway.

That's the instinctual reaction, yes, the conditioned reaction. But I would invite you instead to give yourself permission to open to the fear that's present. Try it. What happens?

Q. There's an opening, a relaxation.

Exactly! It's counter-instinctual, but it's absolutely simple. Anyone can understand this. Simply be honest with yourself about what is, in each moment. Allow yourself to see what is, that's all. It is what it is, in all its infinite richness.

Allowing the Pain of Wanting

Wanting is not the problem; attachment is. There's a difference. Wanting is like the initial reaching or grasping to get something. But attachment is like digging one's claws into it, a tightening, a clamping down of the contraction. That's the distinction. There's a kind of wanting without wanting that ultimately begins to happen, a wanting that is free of any contraction. You can't really practice that, it's just something you'll recognize when it happens on its own. When it's there, you'll see it. You may already experience it in certain ways without even realizing that's what's going on, a kind of ease with what's being given or what's available.

So you learn how to lighten the burden. And the only way to do that is to let yourself feel the pain of wanting. It can be very subtle at first, but once you slow down a little bit—when you come to satsang or go on retreat, or just sit quietly at home—what was really subtle can suddenly become much more obvious. And maybe what you thought was going on turns out to be masking something deeper. Recently someone asked me about guilt. He thought he was feeling guilty about something, but on closer examination it turned out that what he was really feeling was grief. He hadn't realized he was grieving about the recent death of one of his parents.

When we take our surface perceptions too seriously, we can end up on endless wild goose chases that never quite get to the point. So what we find out here is how to actually get to the point. And awareness really facilitates that. Satsang, transmission—what happens here at an energy level facilitates getting to the point. If you're ready, you utilize the environment energetically. It's a powerful working field.

~

Q. I recently had an experience of total attachment like I hadn't experienced in a long time. I was unexpectedly confronted with something that brought up deeply personal material I thought I was long past. There was this sudden painful clenching in my lower abdomen, and a cold sweat came over me. I tried to sit with it, like it was no big deal. I felt I should be able to let my mind do whatever it does and just be above that, but the emotions were too intense. The grief from this old situation was just too much.

The only real problem there is your telling yourself how it should be, how you should be. The fact that grief comes up, even after a very long time, is fine. That it's finally moving is actually very healthy.

Q. How can I stop telling myself I should be a certain way?

By *feeling* what's coming up. By not adding energy to those thoughts. Noticing the thoughts is fine, but be sure to stop and feel what's really going on. What's real is what is felt, not what is thought. Not the meaning we create from our experience. Feeling, really feeling—that's acceptance.

People tell themselves all kinds of stories about how things should or shouldn't be, and in very subtle ways that creates a defense against things as they actually are. So the healing doesn't happen—instead, the difficult material gets stuffed down again, and inevitably emerges someplace else in some other form, sometimes as illness or physical problems.

That's why I sometimes talk about the *ecology of consciousness.* We really do have an internal energetic ecosystem, and what we're doing here is finding out how to manage and support that ecosystem.

~

Q. I feel like I'm really caught in fear and in needing the fear to be gone, and it's hard for me not to judge myself about it on top of everything else.

What are you aware of right now?

Q. As we're talking, my heart feels a little expanded, my head is clearer. There's a certain sadness, or gratefulness.

Yes, there's a healing. There's openness, so the door opens and things move that have been held in. Healing is movement. You're allowing movement, because for the moment you're feeling safe. That feeling of safety, however momentary it may be, allows you to move towards that openness.

Q. I have this tendency to grasp at the openness, to try to hold on to it.

Try thinking of it in terms of intention. Intention is not a grasping towards; it's more like the sun radiating light towards, or a flower emanating fragrance towards. The movement towards openness then is natural, without effort.

Beliefs Fall Away On Their Own

When I was first becoming serious about the spiritual path, around age 20, I found myself at San Francisco Zen Center. I'd read "Zen Mind, Beginner's Mind," Suzuki-roshi's book, and thought, "Hey, this guy sounds like he knows what he's talking about." He had passed away fairly recently when I first went there, and I could still feel his energy. Something attracted me, something authentic was happening there.

So I went as a guest student, and the first thing I asked them was, How long does it take to get enlightened? I didn't want to waste time, and I wanted to know what I was in for. They didn't really answer the question, of course. But I looked around and saw serious-looking people with robes and shaved heads, behaving very formally, and figured, "Hey, they must be enlightened, right?" So I said okay, how long does it take to become a priest? And the answer was "Usually about seven years." So that was it—seven years to enlightenment!

It's amazing what we'll believe, isn't it, the beliefs we allow to run us? I took on those beliefs and they definitely ran me. They ran me to become a monk and go live at the monastery. But the amazing thing you discover, as you gradually find your way on this mysterious path, is that all beliefs eventually change or fall away. Ideas about how long it's going to take, or even the idea of enlightenment itself—at a certain point you realize they're just not there anymore.

Concepts, ideals we believe in or aspire to, can be useful, of course; they can motivate us, and perhaps create a sense of hope or security. That's fine. But eventually they fall away. We don't usually need to consciously extricate ourselves from our beliefs; at a certain point they just kind of dissolve on their own, and gradually we find that there's really nothing left that we believe in.

So how, then, does one receive or relate to so-called teachings, if there's nothing to believe in? What's their purpose? It's an interesting question. Mozart apparently had his wife read him stories to keep his conscious mind occupied and out of the way while he was composing. So maybe we, in a similar vein, listen to teachings to get our conscious mind out of the way so that something else can happen—so the resonance of our being can be nourished, seen, reflected upon, and activated into awakening, into awareness.

So we keep finding our way, in the midst of *not knowing*. There is endless discovery without knowing, an experience of continuous revelation without the contraction into believing. A real, living vitality arises from the willingness to be available to that which is perpetually changing.

If we're hanging on to some way it "should" be, we might not see the door opening. We might miss the door altogether! If we're attached to being a certain way, or to some idea of spiritual attainment, some list of qualities and attributes, we'll keep comparing our experience to the list. We'll be living in a mental world, separate behind a barrier called "my interpretation of reality."

As we grow in awareness and wisdom, however, that interpretation can fall away, and we can experience the great relief of ... not knowing what the hell is happening! And yet awareness, consciousness, energy—that which we are, whatever you want to call it—leads us to the unfolding of truth nevertheless. We become one with energy. We become intimate *as* energy. We become awareness itself.

Feel What You Need to Feel

Spiritual practice only works when there's no one doing it.

There's this ongoing controversy about spiritual practice—whether to meditate or not meditate, the proper role of effort and discipline, and so on. But when there's no one meditating, none of these so-called problems arise. That is to say, when there's no one *taking themselves to be a meditator*, real meditation can happen. If there's still "someone" meditating, then you can have problems. Then you can have controversy.

If you try to figure this out intellectually, you'll just tie your mind in knots. The kind of intelligence this involves really isn't about figuring anything out. It's about being completely perceptive; absolutely sensitive. Then there's no thinking, no figuring out. There's no occurrence of that, no opportunity for it to occur. The light is too bright.

So just be still, and feel whatever you need to feel. Feeling is just feeling! It's just a movement of energy. It's only when we get caught in *who* is feeling that the whole story arises, the whole construct of self appears and creates the illusion of separateness. The ego comes in and thinks, "Am I doing it right? Am I getting it?"

So who's trying to understand what's being said right now? Instead of trying to figure that out, just feel the struggle of needing to know. Feel the push, or the pull, of that needing to know. *That's* the key to peace. All you have to do is be sensitive in this moment—perceptive, not analytical. Analysis might be useful to some degree, as long as it doesn't become compulsive. As long as it doesn't create or perpetuate attachment, analysis is fine. It can be useful. Thinking can be useful. The attitude we have can be useful.

It really comes down to being able to distinguish clearly between reality and projection. That's all. What's the difference between reality as it is, and reality as you think it is? How do you know when you're perceiving reality directly? How do you know you're not projecting onto it your own story, your own conditioning? Sometimes you don't know; sometimes you can't tell. So you fumble along anyway, until eventually the truth becomes obvious.

And when you find yourself in openness—when you find yourself free of suffering, even for a moment—then open to *that*, open to that openness. That's what I would call moving towards the truth. Gradually you'll develop a kind of sensitivity that you can know only through experiencing it. Then what I'm saying will make sense.

So are you open right now? Or are you *trying* to be open? Let go of trying. Feel the difference. The environment of satsang will either bring you more into the peace that you are, or it will agitate that which keeps you separate from it. Satsang really is like a hothouse, and it takes a certain amount of courage to throw yourself into the fire willingly, to bring yourself face to face with *what is* in this moment. The capacity to face *what is* with real honesty is really a power in itself.

It's not about right or wrong, good or bad. It's not about fixing anything—it's about revealing everything. And that revelation precipitates the manifestation of wholeness. This looks like change, but actually it's integration. It's realization.

Q. Don't we always filter our perceptions through our story?

Only until you've come to the end of your rope. That's when true inquiry really begins. That's when you really begin to question. And if you're fortunate, you have the glimpse, the experience of the truth of who you are, and that experience guides you back home. Gradually you come to see that the me, the personal self, is just a function. It was useful for a while, but it's not who you are. That confusion is ended.

It's not like you have to have some big internal war about it; it's more that as you discover and really honor who you are, that which you're not just sort of resumes its rightful place. It's no longer a burden. The identity with ego was the source of that burden; that mistaken identity is really the very definition of suffering.

So keep giving your attention to this openness that you are, and watch what happens. The mystery keeps unfolding, and gradually a kind of intuitive following of that unfolding develops. So dive in, just dive into whatever's present. Words can only point to it. The essence is in the silence—right here, right now. If you're really listening, you can hear the silence. That's enough. Let all these words be in the background somewhere.

Finally, be patient. Patience is really important. Experiencing impatience can be quite challenging, particularly if you've had a dose of the truth. You've had a little carpet ride through heaven, and now you're back in hell. "I've got to get out of here," you may say. "I can't put up with this anymore. How long do I have to put up with this? How long do I have to stay on this rollercoaster?"

Generally what's underneath that is emotional pain—anger, frustration, grief, fear. And gradually you learn to simply allow that pain, allow the energy of that pain to move and pass through and out of the organism. Eventually you stop even asking those questions, because you realize you just don't know. The answers can't be known, and the unknown is the abyss that you learn to leap into.

The Joy of Open-Heartedness

Suffering is not separate from the struggle with what is. When the struggle ends, suffering ends with it. That doesn't mean that there isn't pain, or that there isn't human experience. Obviously there's the whole range of human experience. But the contraction of wanting it to be some other way is gone, so nothing is restricted, nothing is resisted. Things can move.

So just be the space of awareness, and in that openness, you'll find that the struggle unwinds by itself. That openness, that oneness of being, is who you are. Suffering is struggle, and struggle is fueled by ego, the belief that you're somebody. But the truth, that which you truly are, is nobody. It's unchanging. It's not born, and it doesn't die. Understanding this directly is what's really meant by salvation.

As we learn to allow things to move, our conditioning—our "stuff"—becomes food. The crap turns to nourishment. It's like psychic recycling! That's the spiritual path, truly. We're learning how to nurture and care for the ecosystem of our consciousness. It's an interesting process of discovery, isn't it? It's not so easy—sometimes it's painful and confusing. But as we do learn to manage ourselves energetically, to regulate our inner ecosystem with care and compassion, then the heart can truly open.

In the open heart is the true joy of *being*. That's what we are, really, vast heart. The familiar emotional heart is the interface between the body and the true being. So feeling is often a very powerful vehicle for opening into the vastness, the Big Heart. Whatever might be weighing on the emotional heart actually becomes the path itself, the doorway to deepening and expanding. That's why compassion is such an important quality—the capacity to trust what is, to allow what is.

We are all the truth; everyone is, no one isn't. That which we seek is that which we already are. So there's no attainment. We don't have to get it. You can't get what you are, it's already done. The spiritual journey is simply coming to understand that truth, experiencing the shift into realizing what you are and what you're not. That's it!

You can't push it; pushing only keeps it away. So you learn how not to push it while still remaining completely present. Ego is pushing. Ego wants it now! But ultimately you realize you're already it; it's already done. What a relief, to realize *you* don't have to do it anymore! There's nowhere to go, nothing to do, nothing to get. And yet, there's this amazing vastness informing everything in some mysterious way. So you fall into that vastness, expanding into it, deepening into it. Dissolving into it. And all the impurities just keep bubbling up and passing through. All the unfinished business of the body and heart and mind is precipitated, exposed and seen for what it is.

Some people confuse the experience of truth with being in a certain state, kind of like being high all the time, but that's not quite right. It's a bit confused, actually. Any state, no matter how profound or blissful (or painful or unpleasant, for that matter), is something temporary; it arises, does whatever it does, and then goes away again. If you go out to the ocean and stand there for twenty-four hours, things are not going to remain the same. There will be wind, fog, sun, temperature changes, all this movement happening. It's not always going to be sunny and perfect. The weather is always shifting, always changing.

Similarly, you may experience some pleasant state and find yourself trying to hang on to it, but that's still ego operating. Obviously, what you fundamentally are is not something that can be held on to. Can you hold on to the weather? Of course not. Can you resist it? Just as unlikely to work.

Resistance, though, is different from responsiveness. People often worry that if they allow themselves to be open, they won't be responsive anymore, they'll become passive. But that's not what actually happens. On the contrary, you become more deeply, profoundly engaged with life than ever before.

Allowing the Truth to Unfold

How is it possible to be free of suffering, free of the struggle? By direct perception. That's all that's required. Nothing more, nothing less. Freedom from suffering simply means not being identified anymore, which means not being separate anymore. We only suffer when we're identified, and we're only identified when we're separate.

When we perceive directly, there is no separation. There is only perception. What we perceive may be pleasant, unpleasant or neutral; but it is the truth of this moment, whatever qualities it happens to possess. And so we allow, we trust and allow the deepening of our awakening to the truth of this moment, the truth of our being, to unfold in its completely unknowable, unpredictable way.

Our egos want predictability; they want insurance. That's the survival mind, the organism instinctively wanting to survive. And of course there's nothing wrong with that—the survival instinct obviously has its place. But it doesn't cultivate freedom. It cultivates, at best, comfort and safety. And that's okay, actually. Safety doesn't have to be abandoned for you to be free. You can be comfortable and safe. In fact it's probably required, in some sense, for the body-mind to feel secure and safe, so it can be relax and allow *letting go* to happen.

So we sit down, we're quiet for a while. And gradually the unwinding happens—of the mind, and the body, and the heart. And then maybe we get a glimpse, or a taste, of freedom; and if we do, then we give our attention to that. We surrender to that presence. Dropping out of our heads and surrendering to stillness, one-pointed presence, effortless vastness. We let it take us, completely. That's what surrender is.

On the one hand, it gets easier and easier. On the other, it gets more and more difficult, more intense. It's paradoxical, actually. As the water gets calmer, the fire gets hotter. I'm saying a lot of words here, but it's actually nothing very complicated. In fact it's profoundly simple, so simple it really doesn't even require words. The words can be interesting and hopefully useful, and if the words are useful then let's talk. But really, it's like we're just hanging out and having a conversation. Even though you're sitting over there and I'm sitting over here, we can dismantle some of the formality.

If what I'm saying is not making sense to you, or is causing some reaction in your mind or your body or your heart, or something's getting activated and you want to look at it more closely, then feel free to bring it up and we can explore it.

That's not required, though. We can just sit here. The presence in our being together is really the fire of transformation. If you feel that presence, just allow it to happen. But if it's bringing up unfinished energies in you, then feel free to engage, and we'll do our little dialog. Because as you face your truth, whatever that is in the moment, and you're really able to express it, that process contributes to everyone's letting go. That's why it's fun to do this in a group. It's the mutual freeing of everyone. When you're here you can feel it happen.

Presence always activates that which is still unfree. The truth always activates the untrue. Our mind may be convinced things are one way, when the reality is something else entirely. So question your mind, by all means, question what you believe. Question it right out of existence! Because what you believe isn't *true*—it's only belief.

Truth is not believable; truth *is*, period. It has nothing to do with belief. It doesn't matter whether you believe the sun's going to come up or not. It's absolutely irrelevant. Beliefs can be useful for some things, of course. But that's all beliefs are: useful or not useful, functional or not functional. But they're not *true*. To the extent that you believe your beliefs, you suffer, and other people suffer too. Just read the news.

People are sometimes afraid they're not going to be able to function if they don't hold on to their beliefs. They worry that they're going to fall apart, and all chaos is going to break loose. But actually, when you *really* let go of all belief, what breaks loose is profound equanimity.

Discovery

Is it possible to listen to this talk and not think about it? Is it possible to reside in each moment and not be distracted by internal commentary? The key is in being able to distinguish between a purely mental sort of questioning and truly *being available for discovery*. Questioning is very important, but often *how* we ask questions actually inhibits discovery, prevents us from seeing in a new way, from seeing what's actually present.

Discovery is not a mental process. It's a sensory, energetic vibrancy—it is presence, awakened being, the Now. Discovery is surrendering to being filled with this moment, as foreground. That doesn't mean there can't be thinking, but thinking isn't foreground, it's not dominating. It's not controlling, it's not pushing or pulling—it's not struggling. So one way to find out, each moment—no matter what your activity is or where you are—one way to find out if you're struggling is to find out if you can stop, if you can actually stop and *be* stillness, even for a moment.

Being stillness is the absence of resistance, the absence of any kind of restlessness in the body. To truly be stillness, you must be deeply aware in the body. One way to develop that kind of awareness is to use your mental facility—your inner voice, as it were—like a little guide, to direct your attention into your body. Let it tell you, "Feel the feet on the ground; feel the breath; feel that vibration; hear that sound." That way you give the mind something to do, which both keeps the mind busy and is also very useful on a bodily level, because directing the attention in this way redirects energy into the body.

Now you can be available to discover, to awaken in each moment. In that experience, things are absolutely vibrant, absolutely amazing. So-called things are not separate from you, whether they're plants, animals or other people. What's perceived is not static, not separate. There's a deep intimacy, even with inanimate objects.

In the Zen tradition, there's a lot of emphasis on forms and ceremony. I think the intention behind those practices was to energize form. When you're holding the bowl, hitting the bell—it's almost like things become imbued with energy, empowered with energy. Everything we do can be like that. Even the simplest of activities can be empowered with consciousness, whether it's typing on a keyboard, making a phone call, studying, researching; even what may appear on the surface to be difficulty or adversity, like an unpleasant task or a difficult personal interaction.

So we find out how to discover, and it is endlessly amazing. That's the beauty of discovery. It's never, ever, the same. It's always—always!—new and fresh. It's revelation. It's an attitude, you could say—a certain way of shifting one's attention to allow the aliveness of awareness to be cultivated. When we're in discovery mode, gifts keep coming.

Discovery is the realm of Zen mind, which is beginner's mind. It doesn't have a preconceived idea about what's happening. It is not caught in the conclusions of the mind. It is not attached to the beliefs of the mind. It doesn't create more beliefs. The more beliefs you build, the less you're able to discover, until soon enough you're encased in a cement prison. It's like the opposite of Michelangelo's sculpture, "The Slaves"—you're going back into the rock instead of escaping from it!

If you understand *being awareness* experientially, then you also understand what I mean by discovery. It's the same thing. To awareness, each moment is new. Discovering each moment is new means you don't hold back anymore. It means you give yourself fully, you really surrender and allow yourself to be vulnerable and available and intimate with each thing, with each moment. You find out how to really *be* in this moment, however it shows up.

When you drop all your definitions of what you think is happening, you get to receive what really *is* happening. You get to continually discover. As you develop sensitivity in your body, it's like discovering for the first time how it feels to walk, the incredible sensations in your legs, your knees, your feet, your back, your neck, your arms. It's amazing what happens when you awaken the body, and awaken the heart. So much energy goes into the mind, into thinking—too much! To redirect some of that energy and really find yourself grounded and present is wonderful! It's like drinking nectar. It's healing.

Have you ever seen a bird hit a window? Afterward it will just be still and not do anything. It will just be wherever it is, for as long as it needs to be, and then all of a sudden, whoosh! It flies off again. What's it doing? It's being. It's letting the weird, twisted, off-ness find its way back to balance. That's what animals do when they're injured—they hide and remain still. How often do we do that? Not often enough. But it's a great thing to do—it works! I very much recommend it whenever you're out of balance. Otherwise we start struggling with the imbalance, fighting it, which only takes us further from balance.

Enjoy Yourself!

Q. You've often said that the thinking mind is the last to get it. It's always seemed to me that my thinking mind actually grasps something first, then the rest of me catches on later. I'm exposed to a concept first by hearing or reading about it, then later, after I've thought about it, there's a kind of "ah-ha," when it really sinks in all the way.

What I was referring to is that you come to a point where ideas and concepts fall away, where *being consciousness* is no longer about thinking, no longer about identifying with a state or a particular understanding. As you as consciousness move more and more deeply into this mysterious, unknowing realm, the mind may in some sense get left behind. And it may never catch up! In a very real sense, it *can't* catch up; *being* is beyond the conceptual framework the mind operates within.

But I do understand what you're talking about, and I think it's fine to read, and then maybe relate experiences you have to what you've read. There can be a sense of confirmation, then, that you're on the right track. That's definitely part of the process too. The tricky part, though, is that it's very easy for the mind then to think it's understood what's going on, and to try to control through knowing. That can be a subtle form of defense.

Q. You've also talked about self-inquiry, the practice of asking yourself "Who is it that's seeking?" or something similar. Isn't that kind of leading of mental experience an example of the mind exerting control?

That kind of inquiry, properly understood, is not a mental process. It only really makes sense from the perspective of not knowing—from *being understanding*, being presence, being consciousness. Then that kind inquiry is powerful! Otherwise, yes, it can turn into a mental trip that only creates further contraction, and that isn't where it's intended to be coming from.

Q. So you can ask those questions from a place that's not mental?

Yes. Sitting here, notice what you're aware of right now. Notice where your attention is right now. Is it on wanting to understand? Notice what's going on in your body in that process of wanting to understand. Is there tension, or are you relaxed, open? If there's tension, where is that tension? Is it static, or does it change as you bring attention to it? Really enter into sensory awareness, dropping out of the cognitive and into the kinesthetic.

If you persist in this kind of kinesthetic inquiry, what you may discover—and maybe you've already discovered this—is a kind of fullness, or connectedness, or vastness. When Nisargadatta said "I am That," that's what he was referring to. The "That" is not the ego, but the openness of *being*. From the perspective of that openness, the kind of questioning you're talking about can be transformative.

Q. When someone performs that kind of inquiry, asking "Who is being enlightened?" and similar questions, that seems like mental efforting, directed thinking.

Let me put it this way: if the question is asked in the way that it's meant to be asked, it will traject one into vastness. If it's asked from a mental perspective, it will pull one into contraction. By observing the quality of your own experience, you'll know which way you're going. The feedback is very straightforward—it's one or the other. It's the same with feeling. If emotions are truly felt and the energy of emotion is discharged, you'll be more in vastness. If they're not, you'll be more in obsessing and thinking and struggling and pain. So try it, and find out for yourself.

Being consciousness is very dynamic, very alive and very intimate. That's why it's such a pleasure to be here with you. It's like nourishment, food for the heart. If you know what I mean, you know what I mean. Poonjaji always used to say, "Enjoy yourself!" He really meant it. And that's really what we're doing here, learning to enjoy ourselves and enjoy each other. Because when you enjoy yourself, then truly you're enjoying everything, and everyone.

Being It

Q. You've sometimes used the phrase "getting it, " which seems to suggest there's something you can do, some process like meditation, or cultivating compassion, that you can do to "get it." But you've also said that there is nothing to get, that we are already perfect and everything is as it should be.

Right. So your question is...

Q. Well, I've practiced meditation for many years, so of course what I want to hear is that it was useful, and that there is something I can continue to do, practically, that will help me to develop spiritually.

Your question points to a paradox that often comes up in these kinds of discussions. You really can't "get it" in the way you seem to mean; there's actually nothing to "get" in that sense. But at the same time, it can be tricky when you're hearing "There's nothing to get," or "It's already accomplished." What do those statements mean? What do you believe when you hear them? If there's nothing to get, why are you practicing, right? If it's already accomplished, how come you're not profoundly at peace, already free of suffering? That's the conundrum! If it can't be attained, how come you're sitting here meditating? This is an ancient question, really. It points to a very old and ongoing struggle.

It's important to be clear what we're talking about. Awakening is the recognition, even if only briefly, of your true nature. That's a prerequisite. Suzuki-roshi said that spiritual practice *begins* with awakening to your true nature. Then, having had that glimpse, you give *that* your attention, and your intention. Otherwise, what are you doing? Developing really good posture? Getting really good at counting your breath? That's not to say those things are necessarily a waste of time, though; as Aitken-roshi said, enlightenment is an accident, but meditation may make you accident-prone!

Q. Just to comment, when I recently stopped meditating after many years, I felt real relief, because meditation had become such a mind exercise, a constant looking for something. But letting meditation go and just living my life has been a great relief.

Great! That's fine, I understand that. I did many years of intensive practice, and then went through periods of not doing it. It's not about cultivating some compulsive behavior that you do no matter what. However, your question was about the value of these kind of practices. The value of meditation is that it can help you to learn how to *not do*. It's only when there's no longer someone "meditating" that true meditation can happen. Until then there's someone doing something that they're *thinking* is meditation. True meditation is non-doing. Approached with the right understanding, that's its usefulness. Otherwise it only perpetuates compulsive, achievement-oriented mental gymnastics.

Following your breath, paying attention to physical sensations, being mindful and so forth, all can be very powerful tools for developing consciousness. However, if practiced from the wrong perspective they can also strengthen compulsivity, and reinforce being shut down. There's no guarantee either way. It's good to work with a teacher if you have questions about that, and really make sure you're not going in the direction where you're contracting and becoming more bound rather than less.

It sounds to me like you let go of meditation, and that was a good thing. Great! I can totally understand that. However, as you begin to learn how to be present, how to be available, you might consider forgetting this concept called "meditation," and let yourself simply be open to openness. Just sitting, not doing anything. Just allowing. Maybe that's enough. If you want to call it meditation, great. But really, I don't even like the word anymore. It's too loaded. It's become another word like God, or love, or enlightenment. These are very burdened concepts at this point. Freedom—that which you can't get, that which you ultimately are—is free of concepts, free of belief. It's free of those burdens.

Q. I don't know if I'm understanding you. It seems to me that when someone "gets it," so to speak, that actually the concepts do continue to exist. People continue to describe their experience conceptually, so awakening is not really free of concepts.

Well, you can always describe your experience, wax eloquent, write poetry, whatever. And speaking and teaching can resonate deeply with the truth of what we are if listened to from a place of openness. So the concepts aren't intended as intellectual explanations or concrete representations; rather, they're coming from another level—the words are really openness addressing itself to openness.

For me, meditation has been a profound healing practice—physically healing, emotionally healing, psychologically healing—and also a great training in understanding the movement of energy, allowing the cells to begin to integrate and handle a much bigger charge. People aren't living authentically as who they truly are because they're terrified of the energy of that, because it's so vast and so powerful. Meditation can begin to entrain and balance the nervous system so it can handle that bigger charge. People have been doing it for thousands of years. If it's properly understood, it works. Otherwise it's just another thing on the schedule, like yoga class or going to the gym—another "should"!

Q. You say that meditation has been healing, but part of me is remembering other teachers saying there is no "I", there is only oneness, there is nobody to be healed.

That's all true. And yet, if a truck runs over your foot, I'll be very surprised if you don't immediately go to a hospital. Don't confuse the human with the ultimate—they're both functioning simultaneously. When I'm teaching, I'm addressing both. As long as the ego can be acknowledged for what it is, then the truth can also coexist. What you're saying I totally agree with—all those things you hear, those are true. But they can be misunderstood. There's this idea that once you understand the truth, somehow the humanness doesn't exist anymore. That's a load of crap! You still have to eat and sleep, move your body from place to place, and look both ways when crossing the street. And the human organism still needs love and emotional connection.

But here we are. This oneness is right here, right now. This *is* that which is already accomplished, and you're recognizing it. We're here together, recognizing it, as one. This is what I mean by *getting it*. But maybe a better way to say it is *being it*. So we shift from an ego-based struggle to *get*, to simply *being* this openness, recognizing that this openness is what we already are. That's the real value of the teacher—to simply point out that this is it, right now, so that you recognize this openness as that which you are. This, exactly as you were saying, cannot be achieved. It's simply what you already are. From this perspective there's nothing to talk about. We can just enjoy ourselves!

I'm a little more flexible in my language and how I talk about this stuff than some other teachers, and I know it creates a bit of confusion now and then. Even so, I still like to open the conversation up a little, and not have it be so constrained in terms of the kinds of things we can talk about. But I'm really glad you brought this up. I really appreciate the feedback, because I think that when we really dig into these things, we can begin to distinguish experienced truth from some set of ideas about truth and how we should be talking about it.

I'm always learning too—learning how to communicate this stuff continues to be a very interesting process of discovery. In the past some Zen teachers wouldn't say anything; they'd just sit there, and at some point they'd maybe lift a finger. That probably cut out a lot of confusion! People would come to the monastery and not know what was going on, and they'd keep on being confused for a long time. But they'd stick around anyway; that's the amazing part, that we persist. Thank goodness! Even in face of all the confusion, some part of us knows to stay with it.

Resistance Is Just Too Much Effort

Q. I'm having difficulty understanding why one way of experiencing thoughts or emotions is considered "being present" while other ways of experiencing thoughts or emotions are considered "not being present." Aren't we always present either way?

I think you're confusing presence with the practice that's usually referred to as mindfulness. The intentional practice of "bringing attention to" isn't the same thing as presence. Presence is prior to that. Presence is simply that which perceives what is. Presence, or awareness, *is* the perception of what is, and is also not separate from it.

Q. I guess what I mean is there's an aversion to the juice of certain feelings, and I find myself trying to find ways not to experience them.

That's what I thought you meant—the aversion, the struggle. The struggle with what is is absolutely the antithesis of awareness. But if you can see where the struggle is, identify the struggle and feel the struggle, then you're home free. Bring awareness to the struggle, because the struggle is the very center of identity. Turn towards what's difficult. Bring awareness to where the resistance is. We begin to see and experience resistance more and more subtly. It becomes so, so subtle.

Q. For me, though, there's an unconscious agenda that I'm intellectually aware of, which is to use this entire practice to avoid feeling those things.

What are you running away from? What are you trying to avoid?

Q. Unpleasant sensations, basically.

So ask yourself, why? Why avoid them? And gradually you'll see why you do. They may have a certain meaning to you, or they may just be really uncomfortable. Who wants to be uncomfortable?

Nobody! Nobody wants to be in pain. Human beings want to be comfortable. Our nature is to seek comfort and avoid pain—that's human. However, when you begin to feel the pull of truth, there is no longer any possibility of avoiding the dark side.

Q. So then what's the difference between being present and not present?

Well, there's being present as ego, and then there's *being presence,* which is awareness itself. Awareness is the experience of profound openness—the complete absence of resistance. There's no trying not to resist; there's simply no arising of resistance. There's only, simply, openness. And as you become familiar with that openness, that awakened consciousness, you find out how to move towards it, so that consciousness gradually becomes itself. That's what becoming free literally means—consciousness becoming itself, rather than remaining identified with resistance, with ego. This is the real meaning of being present.

So we find out how to let go into this as what we are. And when we do that there's no longer any separation—all of a sudden you and I are one. Everybody here is one. This is not a concept to believe in, or to think about, or to understand. It's an experience that's obvious when it's obvious. If it isn't obvious yet, you may ask me what the hell I'm talking about! Or alternately, you may find it a compelling concept and instead struggle with the thought.

But I think most people who come here have tasted, or have experienced, or are living more and more as awareness. This living as awareness doesn't exclude being human. Both aspects are functioning simultaneously.

Q. I associate the experience of awareness with being deeply comfortable, or even blissed out. So again, when something uncomfortable shows up it reinforces this suspicion that I'm no longer on the right track.

When you experience the bliss or the comfort but there's still something unfinished, it's like the light literally illuminates the dark. So as you cultivate consciousness or light, the energy activates what you've been holding on to or repressing, and that which is most uncomfortable of all emerges, sometimes with great force. That's why it's often said that if you're not ready, there's no way you'll continue; it's just too difficult.

When you begin to understand how the process works, however, you begin to welcome the emergence of this kind of difficult material. When one is established as the awareness that perceives the condition, the condition itself is no longer threatening. That's what *being with reality* really is. That's also what compassion is—the awareness that allows whatever arises to arise. The grief, the fear, the discomfort, the wanting the discomfort to be gone. The wanting to be free! That too. Nothing is excluded. How could anything be? Awareness is infinite. It's all-encompassing.

So there are no bad feelings. There are painful feelings, feelings you may not enjoy; feelings can be terribly painful, particularly when they're tied to very strong beliefs that you're still holding on to, still really gripping. But once you understand the truth of *being with reality*, opening is easy. You find that it's a lot easier to open, in fact, than it is to resist. Ultimately, resistance is just too much effort.

High Expectation Meditation

Q. I recently went through a period where I was meditating a lot, maybe too much. I kind of became over-identified with my meditation practice as a reason for being, and became so physically and emotionally tight as a result of the rigidity I was practicing with that I finally had to stop altogether. Now I'm having a hard time figuring out where to go from here. What does practice really mean?

I often refer to that kind of practice as "high expectation meditation," which is inherently about wanting something. When we're struggling or stressed in some way, whether physical or emotional or psychological, we quite naturally want something that will help, something that will provide relief and comfort. And we hear that meditation can help, so we approach it with that intention: "How do I do this so that it helps me?"

Or maybe we decide to shoot for the ultimate goal of spirituality—we're suffering, but enlightenment is the end of suffering, right? So: "How do I do this so that I definitely get enlightened?" Either way, we set up a kind of goal or set of expectations based on ideas and concepts. Everything we read and hear about meditation can then serve to strengthen those concepts.

But it's very important to distinguish between the form of meditation and the essence of it. Many people can do the form: sitting still, whether on a chair or in some yogic posture. Maybe they follow their breath, or count their breath, or visualize, or chant a mantra, or pay attention to the arising of sensation, emotion, thought, imagery, energy, and so on. Their technique may become very refined, and yet they may not understand the essence of meditation at all.

The essence of meditation is not of the realm of doing, or of becoming, or of expectation. It's not of the realm of belief or conditioned belief structures. So if it's not any of that, what is it? What else could it be? The essence of meditation is of the realm of the unknown. So any idea we have about it isn't it. What we find out is that it's really about allowing, about surrendering, about being present. And in that surrender, we allow what is to be as it is. The essence of meditation is awareness itself, not the *idea* of awareness. To truly understand meditation *is* to awaken.

Now interestingly enough, meditation *practice*—the technique, the form—can facilitate awakening. But that's not the result of effort exerted while meditating. Rather, it's given. It's revealed. It's grace. It's not attained, not achieved. Any effort to "get it" is usually a concealing of it. Any effort that pushes, that is, the kind of effort that's ego based. But there is another kind of effort that's different.

Once one has tasted truth—not the concept, "truth," but that presence of being that is our true nature—then the simple awareness of that presence *is* meditation. If one is still *trying* to meditate, that's not it. That causes more suffering, actually, more tension and contraction. So I would say, relax. Can you simply be present, *as* presence, without an agenda?

Sometimes when we allow ourselves to be present in this way, very difficult material can arise. Remaining present with this awful, difficult, relentless stuff that comes up—that's not easy. Bringing compassion and tenderness to our condition is really important. It's not easy, particularly if we've been conditioned to judge ourselves and make ourselves wrong. To drop all that and allow ourselves to be as we are—*that* is meditation. And then whatever needs to arise—whatever needs to shift energetically, emotionally, physically—will move.

Another way to talk about this is in terms of learning how to care for ourselves, how to love ourselves. I don't mean that in a self-centered, egotistical way; I mean it in the sense of paying attention to what is really wanted by this moment. Are we listening deeply enough to hear that? Or is our agenda in the way? Is the filter of our expectations or our needs blinding our vision?

In true meditation we begin to really listen to what's being asked of us—and it's not always what we've previously thought or believed.

It's really very interesting to begin to live in the intuitive, in the mystery, in the unknown. When you're no longer burdened with the belief systems you've been living from, you find you're also not running away from the reality of your life anymore. Where previously you've been just completely numbing out—and *acting* out!—now you understand what that was all about. "No wonder I did that," you think. You can see the roots of the condition.

It's often very painful, on the spiritual path, to come face-to-face with your core holding point, the core struggle of identity, what I call the *primary contraction*. But that seeing, as painful as it can be, is truly a gift. So can you listen to that? Can you simply let it be what it is, as it is, and not worry about fixing it or figuring it out?

Often when we see through some belief or limiting condition, we immediately try to paste a better belief over the top of it. We effectively try to brainwash ourselves out of our limiting beliefs, or problematic behavioral patterns, by replacing them with better, more functional ones. But the actual opening to freedom is not in fixing our condition or getting rid of it, not in improving it or replacing it or even understanding it. Freedom lies in *profoundly accepting it.*

When I say *profoundly accepting* the condition, I don't mean accepting it psychologically, or adopting an ideology that says the condition is okay. I mean opening to the condition energetically and allowing it to be exactly as it is. True meditation is *being* the awareness that perceives the condition and is not separate from it. *That's* what ultimately leads to enlightenment, to freedom, to living more and more as awareness itself.

And that's what satsang is for—to really make available this presence, this field of being. It may facilitate immediate opening and deepening into spaciousness; or it may bring up and amplify the conditions of holding and resistance. Previously frozen energies may suddenly move, and that may cause physical changes in the body, or emotional upset in the mind. But gradually you begin to look forward to those kinds of shifts. As Rumi says, you become like a moth that looks forward to flying into the fire and burning off its wings. That's not a statement of masochism, that's really a deep understanding of how this process works.

So that's what we have to find out. We have to find out how it works, and then let it. And our conditioning will fight like hell! It's fighting for its life, which ironically doesn't even exist. It's a construct, actually, an illusion. And ultimately we see that. But then we are *not* that anymore; we are awareness itself. That's when one is truly on the spiritual path, when one has tasted or had a glimpse of the truth—when one, in other words, has awakened. The condition, whatever it is, may still be there, but you're no longer suffocating in it, you're not contracted and claustrophobic anymore. There's some space. There's some light. So we begin to find out how to cultivate the light, how to bring awareness to the condition so that the light grows. That's what meditation truly is.

Finding Our Own Way

Q. You often talk about being in the pressure cooker. You say as things come up, just stay in the cooker, and I'm doing that. Sometimes it's okay and sometimes it's less okay, but I'm staying there. And what I'm finding is that all this anxiety comes up, all this fear, and I'm wondering when that's going to end. Is there light on the other side as I move through that? I'm wondering if you experienced that and what you did to move through it.

Your question reminds me of the famous Zen parable about the snake in the bamboo tube. You're that snake, confined in a narrow tube with no wiggle room—antsy and uncomfortable and entirely unable to do anything about it. You stay with what is only when you finally realize there's no choice. Only then. As long as there still seems to be a choice, you'll seek comfort. But once you realize there's no point in trying to get away from this, whatever "this" happens to be, then you stay with it, and you find out how to do that. *You* find out how. Each person finds out how. And that evolves over time in each person, as they find out how to be available, how to truly accept what is. Accepting what is doesn't mean being resigned to what is. It's not a psychological giving up. It is an absolutely profoundly alive engagement with what is.

What's interesting is that as people begin to live more from spaciousness, they sometimes find it challenging to integrate the happiness they find themselves experiencing. Happiness, ironically, can be frightening and unfamiliar when you're not used to it! And if people all around you are still very caught in their struggles, things can get very interesting.

Your attitude towards what's happening is very important. If you're able to question what you're going through, especially your mental ideas and conclusions about your experience, things can continue to move. Otherwise, the defense mechanisms kick in. Conclusions become beliefs, and the body tightens around them.

Satsang really is a hothouse, and people respond to it differently. Some who are available will open, and others who aren't quite ready will feel like running out the door. Or you may be in a place where you're simply not able to face what's happening, so you don't come at all. But please don't give yourself a hard time for having a hard time! If you need to run out the door, by all means run out the door. Or stay home, if that's what's called for. It's important to honor what's actually needed. Laying requirements on yourself just creates more resistance.

So what is it that produces openness, as opposed to resistance? It's not a question of psychology, and it isn't about meaning. It's really a matter of energetic perception. As that perception deepens, the necessary emotional movements can happen. The deep wounds of our childhood or of our later lives can begin to be seen and felt and aired so that they can heal, and we can become whole as beings. We can become emotionally, physically and spiritually integrated.

Q. I get what you're saying about accepting pain, but lately I almost feel like I'm getting a kick out of it, welcoming it in a way. It's almost like pain has become pleasure. I don't necessarily think that's what you're getting at, and it may not even be healthy, but I also think that the amount of processing that can happen when there's movement of pain through me is very useful.

To avoid pain is to avoid pleasure, actually, in the deepest sense. But it's not about seeking pain either. If the pain is there, allow it to move, but don't indulge in it, don't make it some kind of fetish. I'm definitely not suggesting you wear a hair shirt or flagellate yourself, like the ascetics who basically think if they torture themselves enough they'll become one with God. Buddha sort of wrote that one off!

But I do understand what you're saying. In my own process, I got to a point where I looked forward to having my buttons pushed. I wouldn't characterize that as any kind of masochistic impulse; that's not what I'm talking about. But there was a point at which the commitment to liberation became completely foreground, and it became obvious that what pushed my buttons also pointed directly to where there was still holding, to where attention and loving compassion were required. It made those areas conscious. How could I give loving compassion and attention to what was unconscious? I couldn't. But once some difficult thing rose into awareness, once it became conscious, I could embrace that too.

So find out what's still being held back. The willingness to allow what's still in the dark to come out into the light is all that's required. What emerges may manifest physically or psychologically, or as a direct experience of energy or emotion. Transformation can happen in all kinds of ways. We talk a lot about emotional transformation, but that's because we are human, and because most people, particularly in our culture, have learned to live in denial of what they're feeling. So we talk about that, because it's appropriate, it's where people are at. But energy moves in many different ways.

It's so easy to misunderstand this stuff. That's why dialog is important, to make sure we clear up any misunderstandings. And really, it isn't even about understanding, and it's not about believing. It's about *finding your way*. How do you find out what *your* way is, and follow it? Not Buddha's way, or any other so-called teacher's way. The teacher is an illusion. There's no one *out there*, not really. We're all connected at the deepest level. *That*'s what we can trust. Truly, that *is* trust.

Sit with the question. Sit with the anxiety,
the energy of not knowing. *Feel what happens.*

Allowing the Struggle

When we open to the sacred, we become one with the mystery. The sacred doesn't have anything to do with our beliefs—concepts and beliefs only obscure it. So the ultimate question is, how do we become free from the tangle of our beliefs? How is it possible to become free of our beliefs about who we are or what we are, whether those beliefs are positive or negative?

Even the question "How do we become free?" is misleading—it assumes we're not free, and then sets into motion a process of becoming, as if we could somehow, by some effort, achieve a condition of freedom. But is that really possible? How can we become free if we're already free?

In one of Buddha's talks he said something like, "Who's going to untangle the tangle?" But maybe the tangle doesn't need to be untangled. When we're one with the mystery, we let go into *not knowing*. Then the tangle can just be whatever it is, right? Fear, confusion, doubt, struggle; whatever!

So maybe all that's really required is simply to recognize the struggle, to open to the struggle with what is. Not define it, not figure it out, not categorize it; not relate to it, or fix it; but simply, totally, fully allow it, without *knowing* anything about it. Then the heart can open into the mystery. That's all.

Every moment is the truth revealing itself. Even in the struggle and the tangle, the truth is right here. Can we just stop, and allow it to be what it is? That's it really; that's all of it. And as we awaken and taste the truth of that which we are, we see that's its nature—total allowing, total inclusion of everything. It's that simple. It's really not much more than just relaxing, profoundly stopping, and being. Not trying to hold on to a state of bliss—holding on doesn't work! Whatever's here is allowed to be here, even if it's sadness or concern, something we might not necessarily want to feel.

It's okay to be human—in fact it's unavoidable. And it's not a problem! Often people think that to be spiritual they have to somehow transcend their humanity. But in actuality the opposite is true. By really opening to the mystery we embrace our humanity, we become truly human. We allow ourselves our humanity; and similarly, we allow others their humanity and their struggle, and whatever else they need to go through. With others, particularly if we love them, it's not so easy sometimes to allow them their struggle. But that's what compassion really means—allowing what is. That means letting others move as they move, letting them find their way.

The truth sets us free. This mystery that we are is what frees us from the identity of ego, not our struggle to be free. All you have to do is listen and observe and feel what is right now, and not draw conclusions about it. Or if conclusions do arise, recognize them as conclusions, and question them: are these conclusions really true? Of course you always know if you're caught in your conclusions, because you'll feel contracted or separate, restless or agitated. But that doesn't matter—however you are is fine. Whatever's going on will lead you to peace, actually, as long as you're able to really stay with it. So follow what is, not some teaching or some teacher. Just follow what is.

Eventually the struggle drops away by itself. We don't have to somehow make it go away. One day you realize it's just kind of dropped off. Often the mind is very surprised by this. The mind is kind of the last to get it. It wants to be the first, of course. It wants the insurance policy—it wants to check things out ahead of time, and make sure this whole letting go thing is risk free!

Fortunately there's nothing to understand, and it's a real relief to realize that. There's nothing to learn. And yet, learning happens—learning absolutely happens. It's amazing! Learning is the nature of life, the nature of the mystery. How else did these brains figure out how to become brains, these bodies to become bodies? Some amazing understanding unfolded itself. And we *are* that understanding. We are that, and always have been.

It's really beautiful that we can be together in this sacred space. To be able simply to be here—to be exposed, to be unveiled—is really a privilege. Often we're in environments where we're encouraged to be somebody, to live up to an image, an ideal, or an identity. But here we can drop that completely, and just be. That's really precious. And more and more, there are environments where people are allowing that to happen. It's wonderful, and really, profoundly radical.

Embracing Compulsion Without Acting

Q. I recently read something Jean Klein said about moving in and out of awareness, and how there's a kind of organic process that happens between being present and nonpresent. I think I've had this kind of idealized expectation that once you become rooted in being, that's it, you've got it. So when I feel rooted in being for a time but then seem to lose it, I tend to be hard on myself. But I've been noticing recently that sometimes checking out seems natural, like the body's just had enough.

Totally! That's fine.

Q. My concern, though, is that my way of doing that is not always very healthy. I stopped smoking years ago, but for the last month I've been smoking three or four cigarettes a week, possibly more. My sleep patterns have been a little weird and I've been feeling kind of altered much of the time, and I find a little bit of tobacco provides some relief. So I guess my question is basically this: when an urge like that arises, how do I know whether to just sit with the urge, or give in to it?

In other words, when to act out and when not to?

Q. Exactly. How do you know when to let yourself just check out because that's what your system needs, versus making the effort to stay with it even if it feels like too much?

We all experience all kinds of urges—healthy, unhealthy, mixed, and so on. So let's talk about the urges you might personally judge as self-destructive or unhealthy. The simplest thing is to sit with the urge—to really allow it. That doesn't mean you sit there and figure out "Should I or shouldn't I have a cigarette?" Having a mind that can figure things out is really useful when it comes to solving practical problems like why your computer isn't working, but when the question is something like, "Should I or shouldn't I indulge this or that possibly unhealthy impulse," figuring it out rationally isn't always the best approach.

What you're bringing up is really the much deeper issue of so-called compulsive behavior. Things become very, very subtle as you begin to understand this area; you begin to notice this dynamic in every moment, and actually, awakening and liberation are completely connected to this understanding. It isn't about whether or not you have that cigarette—that's irrelevant (though it may not be irrelevant to your health). But ultimately you may just not. I used to smoke, but at a certain point I just stopped. There wasn't any great effort involved; it simply became obvious that continuing to smoke cigarettes was not in my best interest.

Q. That's part of why I'm a little alarmed by this, because I had a similar thing happen. I used to smoke a lot, but then I woke up one morning and there was a very clear voice saying "Stop this." And I did. I didn't smoke for years after that. It wasn't even particularly difficult, I just dropped out of the pattern energetically. But now there's this sense of everything just being really heightened and amplified.

We have a lot of stress in our lives, and often we medicate ourselves with substances. We medicate ourselves with all kinds of things. "Medicate" means soothe the pain. We may also soothe it by eating more, or working more, or buying more.

Q. There's a sense in which things can become strange if you're going through a months-long period where every time you stop and really drop in, all you find is pain. The ego begins to associate meditation and stillness with suffering and contraction. It's weird that when you're really getting deep, you can perceive this kind of endlessness to the discomfort.

That's why it's really important to have good training, to really understand how to use the technology. Meditation is neutral; it's just a technology for paying attention. But applied properly, it can be extremely useful through those kinds of difficult periods.

So you have this urge. Can you just let it be there? Can you *not act* on it? Can you *not judge* it? Can you *not analyze* it? That's meditation. Meditation means *being* what is and not doing anything about it, including trying to understand it. Because "understanding it" is a doing. It's a subtle form of manipulation and control, and it runs most people. You're very present right now. You're in presence. *That's* where you'll get your answer. You won't have to figure it out.

Now if you really want to wake up, it generally is a good idea to avoid certain kinds of drug and alcohol use. That sort of thing can actually prevent awakening from happening, by blocking the emotional flows that need to move in order for the being to really experience opening. No moral judgment there, it's just how it is. In order to really open, you need to be able to access what you're feeling. If you're self-medicating to avoid feeling, you have a bit of a conflict there.

In my own case, I used marijuana recreationally in my undergraduate years. I enjoyed it quite a bit! But at a certain point it became obvious that it was time to drop it. Even when I was no longer using it, however, I noticed that the desire for it still came up. So I allowed myself to have that desire. I didn't lay some trip on myself, like "That stuff's wrong, it's bad, it's gonna mess me up!" That isn't what happened. It was more like I embraced the desire, and at the same time dropped it. So there was no rejection, there was just a dropping away of the need.

Q. I think this is kind of the essence of everything you've told me: don't deny yourself the feeling. If you don't allow yourself to feel the urge, you just keep circling back to it.

Yes, and you just keep acting out! That's why it's called acting out. Acting out implies automatic behavior; it's unconscious. It's habit-mind in the driver's seat.

Q. I get it. I think what's kind of messed up about this whole process is how you keep losing the lesson somehow. When the intensity keeps increasing and there's more and more discomfort, for some reason you doubt that the lessons you learned the last time around still apply.

That's why you need a reality check; and that's why a teacher is helpful. If you're just out there on your own, you can really go off the deep end with that kind of thinking.

Forgiveness Begins With Feeling Completely

Spirituality is really about learning not to resist, and not to run away. You have to start where you are. So can you simply perceive what is in front of you right now? Amazingly, it's that simple.

~

Q. This week I've been thinking about an incident with my father. I was very unkind to him. I've been trying to forgive myself, but I don't really know how to do that. And I wonder if that's what you mean by just accepting yourself. When I was much younger I thought forgiveness meant this: wonderful, spiritual me *will forgive* you. *I even used to do that with myself.*

Most people see it that way. Real forgiveness, though, begins with first experiencing the pain, the hurt, the rage—whatever it was that was never fully felt. When I say "fully felt," I mean completely discharged from the body, not simply gotten over intellectually by convincing yourself that it's finished. The feeling must be deeply and completely experienced kinesthetically, so that the energy really moves.

How do you know when something has really, fully discharged? You'll find there's a newfound sense of openness, of spaciousness; and an absence of contraction, resistance, judgment and pain. Suddenly your perception of the condition, or of the other person, is very different. From that perspective, the perspective of union, there's real, intimate understanding of the other person's suffering, and forgiveness emerges quite naturally. It's not like you're suddenly better or more spiritual than them, or anything like that; rather, it's that you're no longer separate from them at all.

The pain will come out once you've done the energetic clearing. Truly. That's why cultivating awareness is important, because without it you may not know whether you've really cleared or not. No judgment if you haven't, by the way. What doesn't come out now may emerge later. The releasing takes as long as it takes. It can come in waves, as is common in the grieving process; the grief comes, recedes, and comes again, cycling back and forth until it's finally been fully processed.

But more fundamentally, forgiveness has to begin with yourself. In a very real sense, the ability to feel completely *is* the ability to forgive yourself. Once you give yourself permission to feel, there's no stopping it. It's no longer good or bad, it just is. That in itself is a kind of forgiveness for our imperfect humanity. But this isn't an idea, a position you adopt; it's got to be completely embodied, so that you live in the fire of that permission.

That's why what we're doing here is so essential, because what gets cultivated here is pure awareness itself, the essence of the fire. That's why it's said, "Just be *that.*" If you really understand that instruction, then you see everything from the perspective of just being that energy, the essence of all conditions. And really, you do understand. You just need to hang in there. That's why we need each other, really, to help us stay on it.

Q. That feels very clear to me. There seems to be something about this kind of context that makes it easier to meet what's arising and allow it to move through. But when I'm not here in satsang, I tend to take things more personally, and instead of letting them move, I'll just feed them. Then reactivity comes up, and the feelings just get more and more intense.

As you become established in awareness, as you realize that you *are* awareness, it becomes impossible to remain in the contraction of taking things personally. It's just too painful. From that perspective, suffering is literally unacceptable, so you stop contracting in ways that create it. That's the shift that takes place, and that will happen by itself.

Understanding will come only through experience, so it doesn't really matter if you get this intellectually. If you're deepening into awareness, then gradually you see how taking things personally creates contraction, which ultimately strengthens the me, the separate self. As you continue to deepen, you might still take things personally to some extent, but they won't last very long, they won't stick. The contraction will move and release more quickly.

Q. You've said that when we allow ourselves to really feel something, there's a big difference between 99% allowing and real, complete allowing.

Yes, that difference is huge, and very clear from the perspective of awareness.

Q. For me there's this huge investment in being a certain way, and that means not having certain feelings, or only having them for a certain limited amount of time. I can feel that now.

Most people face this: "What does it mean about me if I have this negative feeling or unhealthy impulse?" There can often be a lot of judgment, leading to very limiting beliefs that fundamentally are not true. But ultimately it is all about compassion for ourselves, and about love. When we really find the deep truth, we realize that love is actually all there is.

Self-Acceptance

Q. You recently talked about self-acceptance. I spend most of my time trying to get my friends and other people to accept me, and it's really exhausting. I wondered if you could expand on exactly what you mean by self-acceptance.

What I mean by self-acceptance is the direct experience of reality without resistance, such that you can simply say "It is what it is." It's not good, it's not bad. There's no compulsion to understand it, or to fix it, or to get rid of it. It just is what it is. That's also a description of the recognition of mystery. Each moment is, in actual reality, a mystery; it is not known. But it *is* experienced. So I like to distinguish between conventional psychological self-acceptance, and the more profound acceptance that is *the allowing of direct experience.*

Trying to get someone else to accept you is usually an exercise in futility. I'm not saying you shouldn't express your needs or desires or expectations to someone if you're in relationship with them; but to think that person is necessarily going to change as a result is a delusion. So instead, bring it back to yourself. The result of not feeling accepted, or of not feeling understood, could be an experience of great sadness or disappointment; or anger, frustration, or even fear.

So in terms of what we're doing here, it really isn't about the other person. Not that they don't matter at all; sometimes honest, open, clear communication of what you're feeling is essential in a healthy relationship. For instance, you may feel like you need to tell a friend, "I don't feel like you accept me," and that may be entirely appropriate. On the other hand, you may not have to tell them; you might be able simply to express that in yourself, and allow that expression to bring you into the depth of that pain so it can be experienced and really move.

So how to know what to do? As I've often said, the proof's in the pudding. If expressing your feelings directly to the other feels like it will lead to greater openness and a deeper letting go, then that's the way to go. But if you can see that it would actually lead you into greater defensive contraction instead, then you know the impulse to unload in that way is basically a resistance to what is, and will ultimately create more separation and more isolation if followed through on.

At some point we see that people are who they are. If we're still in a place of needing someone to be some particular way and they fail to live up to our expectations, then quite naturally we grieve. And in that grief you may find that there's an acceptance of that person as they are. That can be powerfully transformative in relationship. It can move things to a whole new level. But again, to anticipate that that will *necessarily* happen is to set yourself up for disappointment.

But this is a great question, a very important topic. Acceptance is a very profound area, very deep. It's really the essence of transformation, of what ultimately engenders true freedom in being. So many teachings point to it. When we fully accept ourselves, then we don't focus any longer on whether other people accept us. If someone tells you your life is absurd and meaningless and a waste of time, you'll hear the words, and they'll be interesting, maybe even amusing. But you'll understand that what they're expressing is their picture, their reality, and therefore actually about them, not you. So you won't be in resistance towards it—and where there's no resistance, there's no suffering.

~

Wanting other people to change is actually a very interesting realm of resistance. We think it's about them, but it's really a trip we lay on ourselves. When you eventually learn how not to lay a trip on yourself, then pretty soon you're not laying a trip on anybody else either. That doesn't mean you can't offer something or be supportive—in fact you may then become more helpful than before. You become the space of awareness and listening—that's much more useful, though the results may not be what you expect!

So be that awareness, and then the listening will be very deep. Everyone needs that kind of listening; when we're suffering we crave that kind of listening, we long for that reconnection. Deep listening can actually provide that. It can even support someone in dying. The greatest support you can give to someone who's dying is simply to be with them in complete openness.

Satsang is truly the space of listening, and as each so-called individual deepens into that listening, you can feel the awareness deepen and expand, and letting go happens by itself.

The Question of Service

From the perspective of separateness, we often desire to help, to fix, to ameliorate; and of course there's nothing wrong with that. It's possible to be of service in that way, clearly. From a deeper perspective, though, we have to think about it a little differently.

From the perspective of non-separation—of union, of oneness—there is no "other" to help, no "other" to fix. Compassion is then simply the natural experience of being with pain, whether that pain is in the body you're walking around in, or in another body.

So I would say that "being of service" in the deepest sense is simply *being*. Not doing something—not being identified with a doer—but surrendering to the pain of the apparent other; the pain of not being able to do anything; the pain of allowing someone else to suffer. This is not callous; this is actually profoundly compassionate. Letting go allows healing to take place, whatever form that healing may take.

If someone is suffering, simply being there with them is a profound service, really the greatest gift we have to give to each other. When you accept the moment completely, you offer them the opportunity to accept it as well. That acceptance is love. It is profound support, profound nourishment. It is the light and energy of life itself. That's the ultimate service.

So being there is enough. In that profound presence, there's no one identified with "being of service." Identity doesn't exist in that realm.

Asking Without Attachment

In our human lives, we often find ourselves in a very interesting balancing act between asking for what we want and letting go of attachment. Some people say that it's very important to ask for what you want—and to get it! And I think most people would agree that getting what you want is fine, and in some sense satisfying. But in and of itself, it's not enough. As William Blake said, "More! More! is the cry of a mistaken soul, less than All cannot satisfy Man." It's the cry of the hungry ghost with a pinhole-sized mouth and a giant stomach—it can never get enough. Trying to fulfill desire can certainly be a source of great suffering.

So how then do you balance wanting and receiving with the simultaneous realization that everything is impermanent? Relationships, health, even our bodies—there's nothing that we "have" that we'll always have, including this life. So what is it that's really important? That's what we're here to discover, and to honor—the truth. The truth is that which is here; that which is permanent, infinite; that which we *are*.

So I think it's crucial to look at the habit of holding on—so-called attachment—whether to views, people, or relationships. As you open into awareness, you'll see that attachment is physiological. It's in the cells. The cells have learned to contract, they've learned to hold. Maybe we feel it as muscular tension, or a knot in our gut. As we deepen in awareness, however—as we realize we *are* that—then we see that the contraction is really a constriction of movement, a blockage of energy. We have all kinds of terms and descriptions for this—defense mechanisms, survival strategies, and so on.

And of course, as we begin to let go, what often happens? Fear! And there are successive levels of letting go, usually, so over time you may have many, many awakenings into profound fear and terror. It's quite normal to experience feelings of disorientation or loss of control, or great fear or anxiety. Those are very natural experiences that come with opening, with letting go, with really deepening. My own first awakening was like that—absolute terror. Profound terror of death. But right there with the fear was something deeper, a kind of tacit "Okay, this."

Letting go might also feel like grief, if it's experienced emotionally. Or you could just feel lost, yet find there is something very poignant, very true about that lostness. Just as fear is the flipside of courage, feeling lost is actually the flipside of arriving home. That's why it's said that the answer is in the question.

So we keep coming back to the source, back to awareness. And then whatever is experienced is seen from that stillness. What's seen can really be all over the place! You get used to that.

But you can't put the cart before the horse and hit the cart and expect anything to happen. What I mean by that is that if you think you can *practice* detachment—well, it's just not really going to work. If you lay a trip on yourself, "I'm spiritual now, and being spiritual means not having attachments," that is itself an attachment to being spiritual! That's actually one of the most insidious attachments, and a difficult one to spot.

What's really important is not so much the attachment itself, but your awareness of it, throughout all the different realms in your life where it can be perceived. Really, that's enough. With that awareness, attachments will drop away naturally. The key is learning how to get out of the way. Initially the ways you block yourself might seem obvious, but gradually you notice and release more and more subtle blockages, until ultimately there's simply no longer anything there in your way, only free-flowing functioning and radiant aliveness. There aren't even the concepts of "attachment" or "enlightenment"—those are gone. There's just this moment, however this moment is. So that's where we start.

Fear is really the communication from your being that letting go is happening. So can you be available to that fear, in every moment that it appears? Every time fear arises, however it arises, surrender to it as much as possible, even if you can only let go a little. My own experience is that as one begins to live more in expanding awareness, the nervous system gradually integrates that expansion and develops the ability to handle that charge. Slowly one becomes established in awareness to the degree that complete letting go is possible without being overwhelmed.

People who want instant enlightenment don't know what they're asking for, really. They want to be free of suffering, and that's certainly understandable. But it takes time for the nervous system to be able to really integrate the loss of identity and not have it be a problem. Generally I think the hardest thing is to have patience and trust that the process is working. It can be very difficult to remain balanced through very, very intense experience. But that's what you keep discovering: you lose balance, and then you find it again. Getting off balance is fine, as is experiencing attachment. You just keep finding your way back, as many times as you need to.

Many people have a tremendous fear of ending up in permanently freaked-out mental states. There's something like a kind of cellular memory, a bodily-energetic residue of things that have happened in the past, and those experiences can be recalled or reactivated by new experiences in the present. So be very gentle with yourself, and learn to not push. You'll actually find that the less you push, the more *it* happens. That's the great teaching and the great revelation, that what awakening actually requires is *no effort*. If you're conditioned towards effort, non-effort can seem quite alien.

At the same time, the mind will say "If I don't exert effort, how will anything get done?" That conflict is what leads people to give away all their possessions and move into monasteries, where (they imagine) they won't *need* to get anything done. But we're on the cutting edge of spirituality, in a sense, because we're saying no to that. We choose to live in the world, to live our ordinary lives in fullness, *and* become free. Talk about prosperity—that's the ultimate prosperity, to be free *and* fully living life. True prosperity is not just getting what you want; rather, it's the ability to fully experience the free-flowing richness of each moment.

It's fine to ask for what you want, but whether you actually get it or not doesn't ultimately matter. If you're resting in the infinite space of openness, you can sort of seed the universe—you can say, "I'd really like [whatever]." You just plant that seed and let it go. As openness, you don't care whether you get what you ask for or you don't. It doesn't matter, and you're not waiting for it. You plant the seed and you forget about it because you know that if it's meant to happen, it will.

But there is nothing wrong with asking. From this perspective you can ask, and realize that the answer is beyond your control. That kind of asking doesn't perpetuate attachment. It's not about wanting, or getting, or having. It's about participating in this creative, amazing, infinite life that we are one with. We are very much at one with the creative process.

So whatever you want, ask for it. Seriously. I mean that in the most profound way. It's very important to honor your desires, and not judge them. And then feel what comes up: "I've got to have it! If I don't get it I'll go crazy!" Whatever arises can then be experienced. That's what's important. Not only will that set you free, it will give you what you *truly* want. Fundamentally, we want to be free of wanting, so we can receive what is—so we can be deeply, gratefully enriched by *now*. This perfect now. That's not a belief, not a psychological viewpoint. That's reality.

You can take anything I say, turn it into a belief, and use it to cause yourself suffering. If you find yourself doing that, I suggest that instead you put it all into a garbage disposal and flip the switch, because any belief you have or develop about spirituality is only going to get in the way.

If a teaching helps you to dive into the truth, then it's useful. If it's not useful right now, *then forget it. Just be here instead.*

Drop That Belief and It's Accomplished

Q. I know there's nowhere to go and nothing to do, and nothing to be except what already is, but I'm curious how I can go about actually living more from that place of identitylessness and belieflessness.

You said it right there—that's the only belief that needs to go.

Q. Which is?

That you need to be coming more from that place. Drop that belief and it's accomplished.

Q. In your own life, what do you do in those moments when you might feel the arising of the identity or a belief, or some kind of contraction?

Once you're established as awareness, identification doesn't stick anymore. It may come up, but it's seen for what it is. It's a movement, really, it doesn't have an existence of its own. It's like a breeze, a vibration. It doesn't have a life, it doesn't stay anywhere. If you find yourself experiencing pain or struggle, or emotional reactions, that's fine, those movements happen. So-called karma is generated only when we try to stop movement, when we grab on to it and try to fix it, understand it, get rid of it, organize it, whatever. But as presence, you're just the space within which the movement happens.

As the identity with ego gradually falls away, you'll notice the absence of certain patterns that used to run you. It's not like you intentionally got rid of them somehow; you just suddenly notice they're not there. "How interesting," you think, "my buttons aren't being pushed." You just notice that. It's not like some accomplishment—it isn't even a big deal. It's almost a non-event. Really, it's extraordinarily ordinary. It couldn't be any more ordinary. And then the profound is seen in everything. The so-called mundane is absolutely sacred. But it's not special! It's not a big deal. You can just be at ease.

Q. Is there any point in putting attention on the dissolution of fixations? How does one untangle them? It seems like what you're saying is that there's nothing to untangle, there's nobody untangling anything, and there's nowhere to get to.

That's right. If there is a so-called contraction, it will simply unwind by itself as it comes into awareness. But when faced with an emotionally powerful experience, our conditioning is usually to contract, to stop the feeling. So often people have to relearn how to feel, which means learning to get out of the way and allow the movement of feeling, which can be nothing less than terrifying if it's not how you're accustomed to being. Surrendering in this way may feel like dying, in a sense, or completely losing control. But once you've gotten through it, it's an enormous relief, like taking off a tight shoe.

Spiritual maturity means not looking outside oneself anymore. Sure, coming to environments like satsang, where awareness is mirrored, is great. You can enjoy that. It's a kind of saturation, which is nice, and very useful. In my case it was essential! But don't then think that awareness is outside you somewhere, that someone else has it and you don't—that can be very disempowering. Be grateful for your teachers, and benefit from your interaction with them, but also know that which they're reflecting is that which you are.

And once that is revealed, honor that revelation, and trust it. Sometimes it's very difficult to trust, particularly when you're struggling. Sometimes people feel that they had it but have now lost it, and experience great upset as a result. But really, it's not possible to lose it—how can you lose what you are? You can lose sight of it, maybe; you can be blinded or distracted by something else.

Q. So when I get lost, when there's no recollection of awareness, when ego, or whatever word you want to use, is totally enveloping—in the middle of that darkness, what do I do then?

I think Suzuki-roshi put it very succinctly: "Sit with what is." That may not be so easy. You might want to scream, or wail, or tremble in terror. Sitting with fear—not controlling it, but really letting it be—can be overwhelming. But at some point we take that leap, and we find out what's true: that we can surrender, even in the midst of the darkness. And then the next time it's a little easier. Fortunately you know who you are, truly. That's the real saving grace. The infinite is the ultimate safety net! You can let go and drop.

Being Free Means Not Knowing What's Going On

The dissolving of the ego can be very uncomfortable. People want freedom, but they're also afraid of change, afraid of the unknown. You want to be free, but you also want to know what's going on. But being free means *not* knowing what's going on. So drop out of time. Drop out of the future. The future is a mental world, it's not real. Reality is *now*—the infinite now. The analytical mind can't wrap itself around it. Give your mind a break, have a little compassion for the poor thing.

Some friends and I were just talking about Halloween. It's so interesting, people *love* Halloween. It's this amazing time where you can put on a costume, assume another persona and become someone else, and it's liberating. Isn't that interesting? We're doing something like that here—but we're taking it off! We're taking off the costume and the mask, and it's even more liberating. We get so constrained in our identities. We get so invested in who we think we are, or who other people think we are, or who we're supposed to be, or who we want to be. All of that takes so much energy.

Q. What is the glue that hooks us into wanting to be who we are, who we think we are, this illusory ego self? What makes it so sticky?

The need to survive! We're thinking beings, but we're also animals with an instinctive drive to survive. That drive also produces the violent aspects of humanity, which we're unfortunately quite familiar with. The ego is a natural outgrowth of the survival instinct.

Q. In what way is it an outgrowth, how does it evolve? There's that instinct in animals too. Why are humans so different?

We're human beings, and we are *also* animals, and we do have instincts to survive and to be loved and to belong. This is part of human psychology and human nature. But we're not just human nature, we're also infinite consciousness. As we become more conscious, we begin to really see our humanity in all its unconsciousness. And it can be appalling! People kill themselves because they can't stand it.

But awareness, by its very nature, is acceptance. I don't mean the *attitude* of acceptance, but rather acceptance without an attitude. That's the transformer. That's what moves identity from ego to liberation. It's that simple. Grace happens instantly, though you may then go in and out of it for a while until you're done, until identity is freed from the condition.

As You Realize It, Move Towards It

There are so many different descriptions of grace, transmission, revelation, so many different ways we've expressed that extraordinary aspect of life. That which we are is grace. Grace is another name for spacious awareness, or vastness. When we initially realize what we are, it can feel like we receive the realization, like there is a transmission that comes to us from outside ourselves. But really, it's more like the ocean entering the ocean. That's what happens in satsang.

That's why satsang can be a very rich environment when we're here together. Some people describe this richness as an amplification of the vastness, but it's really just the Self seeing the Self. As you experience it and move more into the truth of what is, it seems to fill you, which can feel like grace, or transmission. Or joy! There is an energetic quality to it, certainly; it can be experienced in many ways.

So as you realize it, move towards it. Otherwise there's still a passive kind of orientation—it can feel like something is being done to you by someone else. That's okay at a certain stage, but eventually there's a maturing that happens where you realize that no, it's not coming from out there. It's like going from being in the presence of a realized person to *being the presence*, period.

Of course, presence can be reflected by a so-called teacher, and that can be useful; teaching environments can be very useful. You see the mirror, and the mirror is useful. But the mirror is everywhere, actually—everywhere, in everything. Ultimately there's nothing that doesn't transmit the truth. There's nothing that isn't filled with grace. Of course, that's a fairly rarified perspective—it's definitely not a concept you should try to believe!

This is what's meant by "The truth will set you free." The recognition of truth is what frees consciousness from the identity with ego. This truth that we are, spacious vastness, is the truth that sets us free, not some concept of truth that we believe in.

~

Q. I've been watching you do your work. It seems that what's most important is the attunement, the resonance between you and the person you're working with. In those silent moments of transmission, of profound connection or presence with another person, what do you experience inside?

In a way it's perceived through the body. But at the same time it's much vaster than that; in fact it's infinite. It's like being the weather. It's like becoming the wind, or becoming the sun. It's really union with the life force. And though it's not willed, there is, in that, a kind of guidance, an intelligence that functions.

Q. Do you turn on some kind of force?

No. Language is very limited here, but I would say that what happens is intimacy becomes intimate with itself. There's no separation. And yet it's not like merging in an inappropriate psychological sense, as when people become unhealthily enmeshed. I think it's actually beyond explanation or description; it really is a mystery. But I also think the mystery reveals itself. As you deepen into awareneness, the revelation of how it moves and works presents itself in each moment. Concepts and conclusions are perhaps helpful in talking about it, but are definitely not something to believe in, or to try to apply in an effortful way. Each person finds the truth in their own unique way.

There's an element that I'd say revealed itself when I had my first awakening in this life, which was around age 17. There was a feeling of being guided that opened up then. In a sense that guidance has never gone away; it's just gotten more inclusive. I once asked Jean Klein about this: if the student is deeply available to hear the truth, is the truth automatically given? His answer was yes. Yes it is. There's no way it can *not* be given.

At the same time, transmission can easily be misunderstood. People sometimes get the idea that they just need to get zapped more by the teacher, that they need some kind of shakti amplification. And physiologically, in the body, it can certainly feel like something like that is occurring on occasion. You can experience profound altered states, physical movements, all kinds of energetic phenomena. But in the most fundamental sense, all of that is beside the point.

The truth is that often in satsang, if someone is getting in touch with their issues, their pain, and they're really on it, the space of the whole room seems to expand with the energy being released. If you're living or perceiving as energy, you feel it. It's like all of a sudden there's more light, more energy.

Q. Do you consciously choose to be connected to oneness in order to be of service to someone in need? Do you make a choice to be of service?

That's an interesting question. But no, service just happens. There used to be a choice, but not anymore. It's no longer personal. Choice is personal: *I'm* doing it, *I'm* not doing it, *I'm* getting the results. But there's none of that anymore, that's all gone. There's only the function, which happens by itself.

Certainly there used to be the position of being of service, as it were. But even though there's still the recognition of that role—obviously service happens, and there is a certain sense in which one can perhaps focus or defocus one's attention—there isn't an identity with it, it's not held onto as a conceptual position. If we come here and what we experience is an amplified focus, it can be useful functionally, and that's what matters.

All I can say is it gets more and more far out. Everyone I know who's generally in this realm agrees with that. We're all kind of like, "I have no idea what's going on, but it's pretty interesting!" I guess you could say I assume a certain role, in some sense; but really, more fundamentally, I don't. It would be too much of a burden, actually. It would be too much to hold up. It wouldn't even be possible! There's really no one who's doing anything, and there's no difference between you, me, or anyone. We're all equal, truly, in the deepest sense.

And that's what's perceived, actually—enlightened beings, every one. What's also perceived is people's resistance, their pain, their energetic holding and emotional stuckness, and so forth. But that's just the human element. Obviously there are times where the human element seems problematic. But really, how can you separate the human from the spiritual, how can you say which is affecting which? What's really being sought is balance. The greatest healers are people who facilitate getting out of the way of healing. So how do *you* get out of the way of what needs to be balanced?

The truth is that as you move more and more into awareness as who you truly are, you see that awareness in other people as well. And when you see them as who they truly are, that allows them to see themselves as who they truly are. And *that's* the true transmission, the true movement of acceptance. There's also a listening that develops, a receiving of what's being given. That listening is endlessly amplifying itself. I can't exactly explain it, but it really is a kind of endless expansion into light and love and wonder.

The Field of Presence

It always fascinates me how, once we've been together for a little while, there's a kind of gelling that takes place, like the tuning of an orchestra. At first everything's discordant, out of sync, but at a certain unpredictable point it just comes together. So even though we seemingly arrive here as individuals, there's another level at which that's not really what's happening.

The understanding of that is the recognition of the unity of consciousness. Sometimes it happens for you right away—you get here and immediately you plug right in. On other occasions it may take some time for you to relax and open. Or you may open through the process of walking into the fire of some resistance.

Even though there may be only one person involved in a dialog at any given time, that dynamic actually includes everyone here. So you begin to listen, not from a place of intellectual analysis, but from open-heartedness—as awareness perceiving awareness, that open, unencumbered listening, that exquisite clarity. It really is that simple.

This can of course be destabilizing if you're holding on to something, if you're protecting yourself with a shield of separateness. That kind of contraction could become agitated in an environment like this that facilitates openness and expansion. If that does happen, it may feel like something external is bugging you, rather than something internal. Or your core issues may suddenly arise, whatever they happen to be—physical, emotional, psychological, whatever. And that's okay!

Another aspect of the experience of contraction is that the mind will often create some meaning around it, some story. This is a further distancing from the fire of transformation, from that energetic agitation which is really inviting opening, inviting surrender; inviting stillness, which is our nature, fundamentally. So you have to find out how to enter the flame, how to dive into the fire—not as if you're engaging in some kind of self-flagellation, but rather in the understanding that in the fire is purification, the transformation of held energy into free energy.

It's really all energy—all of it, everything. Now that's a cool concept, and of course it's great to be thrilled by a mind-blowing concept. But to actually *become* that energy, experientially—that's the journey that we're on here. Becoming *that*. That's where we're explorers and scientists together, discovering the unknown moment by moment, allowing the unknown to reveal itself. And not getting caught in what it means or doesn't mean! That's always a diversion.

But don't believe what I have to say. Check it out! This isn't about believing anything, it's about seeing it for yourself. The truth is directly available to everyone, always. It may be obscured; when it's raining or foggy, the sun and sky are obscured. But the sky is always present, and eventually the fog clears.

So there is an advantage to coming together like this and allowing a sort of amplified field of awareness to arise. We find out how to dive into this space here, how to drop body and mind. It's so wonderful to be with you, with so many people who are so mature spiritually and have done so much work on themselves. It's a great pleasure to share this with you.

So how do you really dive in completely? By not getting caught in, or distracted by, resistance. And how do you do that? The answer's too simple: By *doing absolutely nothing*. Absolutely nothing. That doesn't mean checking out, or spacing out. It means being 100% present, but interfering with nothing: not with thoughts, feelings, perceptions or energies. No interference; no manipulation; no resistance.

That's why sitting in stillness can be very useful, because usually we're so busy, so active, so *on*, that we don't have the opportunity to notice all the ways we resist. So it's very helpful simply to stop and pay attention. Not to try to meditate; not to *try* to do anything. Instead, find out what *wants* to try. Actually discover that which is trying to get it. Because "trying to get it" is all that's in the way. How can you get it? You can't get it. You *are* it.

The proof's in the pudding. When you truly *allow,* then awareness moves to the foreground. I think most of you know what I'm talking about. You've experienced it. You've tasted that truth, that vastness. That's your biofeedback, if you will. Now follow *that,* give that your attention. Awareness will engender awareness; light will engender light; light will illuminate dark; and dark will become light.

I often use the example of putting an ice cube in a bowl of warm water. At first the ice seems separate from the water, but as it melts, you see they're really the same substance. So that which looks dark, that which we think is wrong or bad or has to be fixed—the essence of that is also light. So everything is recycled. Everything. Whatever you think isn't, that's the thing to look at. The one thing you think shouldn't be there, the thing you're trying to stop, trying to get rid of? That's it. That's where to put your attention.

It could even be a little trickier than that. The core issue might *seem* to be the thing you're trying to get rid of, but the real problem might actually be the *trying* to get rid of it. So the seeming problem itself isn't the real problem; the resistance to it is. Say for instance someone is experiencing intense fear. They feel the fear and it's very difficult and painful. So naturally their focus is on the fear itself, but at the same time they *really don't want* to be having the fear, and *that's* where the real resistance is. The problem isn't the fear, it's the *not wanting* it.

So ask yourself, what are you pushing away? Can you perceive in your body, kinesthetically, what you're pushing away? Or what you're trying to pull towards you, or hold onto, or understand. Bring attention to that pushing or pulling. There's your path, that's where you'll find your work laid out for you.

It's so perfect! You don't have to read any books or understand anything. This doesn't require intellectual understanding, it requires getting your feet wet. It requires getting your hands into it, getting your whole body into it. Getting your heart into it, your being into it.

~

Q. I've really been struggling tonight. Yesterday I felt really open-hearted, and then today something happened and I drew in and shut down. I'm feeling afraid, judgmental. When you talked about feeling the resistance, I realized how hard I'm struggling with my fears and dislikes. So is that when I have to feel the not wanting, the trying to change?

Yes, exactly. Another way to put it is, be aware of the doer, the one that's trying to do something about the resistance, because that's the contraction. Can you simply be the awareness that perceives that trying? You don't have to do it, you don't have to try. There's nothing you have to do. So can you do nothing right now? It doesn't quite work, does it? Can you *do* nothing? Of course not. But can you just be here? Can you just let everything be? You can. Stay with it.

Q. There's fear.

Of course. So can you simply let the fear be there? You're finding out how to be awareness. The temptation is to *try* to be awareness, but that doesn't work. That only creates more resistance, which brings to the foreground the conditions of fear, isolation, judgment, and so on. So gently, very gently, just let it be.

Q. I can feel the trying, I can feel it right there.

Stay there with it. Don't abandon yourself. Forget about me, or anyone else. Stay right there with what's asking you to pay attention. Don't go outside, stay right inside. Right in with yourself.

The Realm of Blessing

When you're truly open, you can plant seeds of intention in the fertile ground of Universal Mind, of Big Heart. You can plant blessings for healing, for freedom, or to receive whatever help you might need. Planting seeds of intention in this way is not about "I want something." It's not about ego. It's not about anticipating or expecting. It's not about needing. It's possible only in the space of openness. When you're intimate with the mystery, seeds of intention are planted instantly, and then you forget about them.

This is not an intellectual or psychological or conceptual process I'm talking about. A blessing or question or intention planted in this way is something offered into and received by openness, by the resonant field of spaciousness. You'll know when your expression is received, because as you say it, as it's done, you feel an expansion—an amplification of the vastness, just like in satsang.

We're in the realm of blessing. The realm of openness *is* the realm of blessing. You can enjoy it for what it is, in the moment, or you can explore it. A few years ago I was in Sedona on personal retreat. My father had just died, and it came to me suddenly that I needed my own retreat, my own hermitage. Without any conscious intention, a seed was planted. That very day I checked my email and a place had become available. A small cottage was offered to me in Bolinas, and it became my personal hermitage for several years. So be careful what you ask for in the deep space—you're likely to get it!

Most teachers don't talk about this too much. Usually people just talk about, you know, freedom. And that's cool! Freedom is good. But it's not the end. Freedom is only the beginning. That's when *everything* is beginning. Everything is fresh, everything is new.

So when you find yourself in openness, explore planting seeds, and see what happens. I don't mean engage in wishful thinking; that's not what I'm talking about. That's delusion, that's ego. This is something different. The reason I'm talking about it is that so often in spiritual circles we hear the mind described as this intensely negative burden, as if it's some kind of enemy or beast that needs to be tamed, or chained, or at least sent to finishing school. But there's another level of mind that is both the realm and the expression of the vastness and the mystery, and we are one with that as well.

You'll know when you're resonating on that frequency, because when mind moves you'll feel the connection. Maybe you'll write poetry, or paint, or dance. We know when we're plugged into the creative force—we feel it. You often hear writers say things like "The book just wrote itself," or "It just came through." It's what athletes mean when they talk about being "in the zone." It is true surrender, merging with the creative force. That's what we're playing with here, that's what we're exploring. That's what we're becoming intimate with.

It's easy to get distracted by the demands of survival, or our need for comfort, or our desire for entertainment or stimulation. But now we've gotten a little quieter, a little more at peace. So I invite you to explore the vastness of the mind. Plant some seeds. Find out.

Acknowledgements

I want to begin by thanking Brother David Steindl-Rast, Jeff Foster and Adyashanti for being the true, loving and supportive friends that they are, and for generously writing and offering their endorsements and Foreword, respectively. Thanks also to Julian Noyce for publishing the book and being a joy to work with.

Sincere gratitude to the following for their roles in making this book a reality:

Kenton de Kirby, Dyan Ferguson, Ayoung Kim and Chris McKenna for their invaluable help in reading and commenting on earlier versions of the text; Coulter Boeschen and Kenton de Kirby for their consistent, weekly audio management and recording of my events year in and year out; Jason Miller for additional audio support and technical advice; Ahmed Khouja for help with the cover design; Kenneth Haugan, Lee Zipin, Ayoung Kim, Kathryn Hirt, Liz Coleman, Mira Hess, Lar Bryer and Greg Taylor for carefully transcribing the recordings from which the text was adapted; and Mark Peters for being the Hostess with the Mostess at Monday night satsangs.

I especially want to thank my dear friend Kenneth Haugan. The mere existence of this book is in large part due to Kenneth's extraordinary commitment to a project which has extended over a number of years. He has not only skillfully managed to transform what appears in the spontaneous and vibrant environment of "teaching" and made it accessible in written form, but has edited and organized the entire manuscript. And if that wasn't already more than enough, he managed the entire team previously acknowledged. I am deeply and profoundly grateful for his efforts.

NON-DUALITY PRESS

If you enjoyed this book, you might be interested in these related titles published by Non-Duality Press:

Eternity Now, Francis Lucille
The Wonder of Being, Jeff Foster
An Extraordinary Absence, Jeff Foster
Awakening to the Dream, Leo Hartong
From Self to Self, Leo Hartong
Dismantling the Fantasy, Darryl Bailey
Standing as Awareness, Greg Goode
The Transparency of Things, Rupert Spira
Perfect Brilliant Stillness, David Carse
I Hope You Die Soon, Richard Sylvester
The Book of No One, Richard Sylvester
Awake in the Heartland, Joan Tollifson
Be Who You Are, Jean Klein
Who Am I?, Jean Klein
I Am, Jean Klein
The Book of Listening, Jean Klein
Spiritual Discourses of Shri Atmananda (3 vols.)
Nobody Home, Jan Kersschot
This is Always Enough, John Astin
Oneness, John Greven
Awakening to the Natural State, John Wheeler
You were Never Born, John Wheeler
The Light Behind Consciousness, John Wheeler
What's Wrong with Right Now?, Sailor Bob Adamson
Presence-Awareness, Sailor Bob Adamson
You Are No Thing, Randall Friend
Already Awake, Nathan Gill
Being: the bottom line, Nathan Gill

For a complete list of books and DVDs, please visit:
www.non-dualitypress.com